Michael Price & Sue Price

Internet
for Seniors

For the Over 50s

In easy steps is an imprint of In Easy Steps Limited
Southfield Road · Southam
Warwickshire CV47 0FB · United Kingdom
www.ineasysteps.com

Windows Vista Edition

Notice of Liability
Every effort has been made to ensure that this book
contains accurate and current information. However,
In Easy Steps Limited and the author shall not be liable
for any loss or damage suffered by readers as a result of
any information contained herein.

Trademarks
All trademarks are acknowledged as belonging to their
respective companies.

Printed and bound in the United Kingdom

ISBN-13 978-1-84078-356-8
ISBN-10 1-84078-356-7

Contents

11 Publish to the Internet — 151

12 Internet Security — 169

Website Directory — 179

Index — 187

1 Get Started

This chapter outlines the Internet and the World Wide Web, discusses the facilities you need to get on the Internet from your computer, and introduces the latest version of Internet Explorer, that gives you safe and secure access to the Internet.

The Internet

Beware

There is no overseer or manager for the Internet, so Internet security is provided by software installed on your computer (see page 170).

8

Hot tip

The computers on the Internet are known as hosts or servers, and create exchanges for news, views and data of all kinds.

The Internet (**Inter**connected **Net**work) is a global network connecting millions of computers, organized in thousands of commercial, academic, domestic and government networks and located in over 100 countries. The Internet is sometimes called the Information Highway, because it provides the transportation and routing for the information exchanged between the connected computers.

The computers on the Internet are connected by a variety of methods, including the telephone system, wired networks, wireless (radio) networks, cable TV and even satellite.

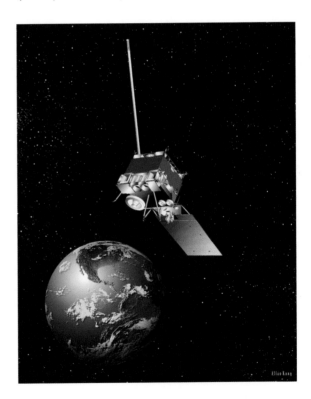

Some sections are commercial, others are academic or government, and no single organization owns the Internet as a whole. It is simply made up of the individual, independent networks and computers, whose owners and operators decide which Internet methods to use and which local services to offer to the global Internet community.

Internet Services

The services offered could include one or more of:

- **Electronic mail (email)**

  This allows you and other Internet users to send and receive messages.

- **FTP (File Transfer Protocol)**

  This allows your computer to retrieve files from a remote computer and view or save them on your computer.

- **Internet Service Providers (ISPs)**

  These, as the name suggests, provide points of access to the Internet. You need an ISP account, plus the means of connecting your computer to one of their computers.

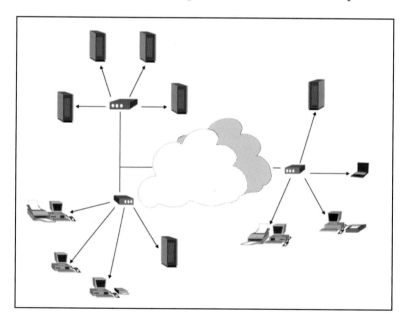

- **World Wide Web (WWW)**

  Also known as the **Web**, this is made up of collections of files and documents that may include images, animation, video and hyperlinks to other documents. These can be on the same computer, or on different computers, anywhere on the Internet.

Don't forget

There are other ways to connect to the Internet that don't require a computer, such as cell phone, or a PDA device.

Don't forget

A location on the Web is known as a website. It will have a home page, the document that you see when you enter the site. It might have additional documents (web pages) and files, usually related to the main theme or focus.

Hot tip

To visit a website and follow the hyperlinks in the web pages you will need an Internet browser (see page 14).

Hot tip

If you are planning to access the Internet from someone else's computer, it should be already set up for Internet access, though you will need the sign on code and password for your email account.

Beware

Don't assume that your supplier will have provided the best choice in every instance. Often, there will be 90 day trial versions of software, or lite (limited function editions) and you must pay extra for the full product. You may find cheaper alternatives and even free options, if you search on the Internet.

Requirements

To connect to the Internet, there are a number of things that you'll require:

1. A computer equipped for use on the Internet. In this book we assume that you are using a Windows-based PC (see page 11)

2. A means of connecting your PC (or PCs) to the computers at your ISP, including the hardware components, the communications software and the cabling or phone links

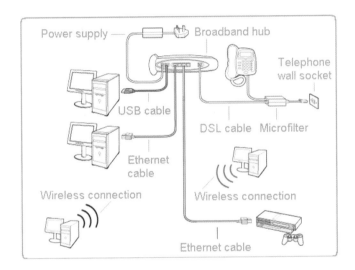

3. An ISP account that will provide access to the Internet. You may also need email services, which would normally use the same account

4. Appropriate software on your computer, to exchange information with other computers on the Internet, and to send and receive emails

We'll look at each of these in turn, so you know all the tasks that are involved in setting up your computer, and can identify what remains to be done.

Internet Enabled Computer

If you purchased your computer within the last three or four years it will almost certainly be adequate for most activities on the Internet. If you have an older computer, review these hardware and software specifications to see if it will meet your needs for Internet access.

Processor
If your computer has a Pentium 1GHz processor or anything faster than this, you won't be restricted by the power of your computer.

Operating System
While any version of Windows will allow you to access the Internet, for the best security you should upgrade to the most current version, e.g. Windows Vista. The Home Premium or Ultimate editions are recommended for home users.

Memory
Although it is possible to run your computer with less memory, your use of the Internet will be smoother and more effective if you have memory of 1GB or more installed.

Hard Disk Drive
Check the free space on your hard drive. If there is 20GB or more available, you'll have no problems with disk space. Any less, and you might wish to consider replacing the drive, or simply adding a second drive.

Display Monitor and Adapter
To take full advantage of the Internet, you should preferably have a monitor 17" or larger, capable of displaying Hicolor (16bit), Trucolor (24bit) or better, at a resolution of 1024 x 768 pixels. CRT monitors and flat screen LCD displays are equally suitable, though the latter are much easier to house.

Don't forget

Other requirements include a soundcard, speakers and DVD drive, if you want to play videos on your computer. You may also want a printer and perhaps a scanner, but these are not essentials for accessing the Internet.

Hot tip

To check the computer specifications, open Control Panel, click System and Maintenance and then System, to see the operating system level, the processor type and the memory installed.

Don't forget

Open the Computer folder and select the individual drive to check the size and the space available on the drive, displayed in the Details panel at the foot of the window.

Connection Types

The type of connection you need depends on how much use you will be making of Internet access. There are four main options, though not all are available in every region.

Dial-up

This is a low speed, low cost method for limited usage (less than say ten hours per week). It uses a Modem in your computer, which connects to a standard telephone socket. Your normal phone line is unavailable for incoming or outgoing calls while you are using the Internet.

DSL Broadband

This offers higher speed and supports a higher level of usage. It uses a DSL modem attached to your computer or alternatively a separate device known as a router. It makes use of your telephone connection, but transfers data in a digital format that allows the line to remain available for normal incoming or outgoing calls. You can if you wish leave your computer connected all the time.

You must check with your telephone company to see if DSL Broadband is available in your area.

Cable TV

If your area has Cable TV services, these may offer a broadband connection. This operates in a similar fashion to DSL Broadband, but independent of your telephone line.

Satellite

Internet via satellite services can provide you with a permanent 2-way connection to the Internet that uses no telephone line. All you need is an interface box and a small satellite dish connected to your computer.

Wireless

This is the type of connection you use with a laptop computer (or a handheld unit) when you are away from home, at an airport or hotel. Your computer has a radio modem, and the organization you are visiting provides the hub device which in turn connects to the Internet.

Hot tip

You may pay as you go for the call or connection time, or pay a fixed fee for a specified maximum number of hours, depending on which works out most economical for your average amount of usage.

Beware

You may have a Wireless connection with DSL Broadband. This still uses the normal telephone cables to connect to the ISP, but allows you to access the router from anywhere in your home. However this is not full wireless connection.

ISP Account

Having decided the type of connection that meets your needs, you need an Internet Service Provider to complete the connection. There are several ways to identify ISPs:

- Ask friends and family which ISP they use

- Check for pre-installed links on your computer for setting up a well-known ISP, such as AOL or MSN

- Look for CDs for ISPs in the information supplied with your computer, to get onscreen instructions

- Check at your local bookstore, supermarket or computer store for ISP CDs and special offers

If you have access to the Internet on another system, visit a website that can help you choose a suitable service., e.g.

1. Visit **http://www.theispguide.com/** for details of North American providers

2. For UK services, visit **http://www.ispmenu.com/**

Don't forget

You need to make sure that the ISP provides a local telephone connection number, if you are using dial-up. For broadband, check that the ISP supports the type of broadband you will be using.

Hot tip

Your selected ISP may provide modem, router or other hardware components needed to set up a broadband account.

13

Don't forget

Choose a website that provides a directory of ISPs for your particular country or region.

http://www.ispmenu.com/

Internet Browser Software

Don't forget

There are other Internet browsers, such as Firefox, Netscape and Opera. The layout may differ if you have something other than Internet Explorer, but you still should be able to take advantage of the suggestions and examples in the book.

Hot tip

IE7 protects you against the theft of personal data via fraudulent emails and fake websites, the practice known as phishing. See page 171 for details.

The software used to access the Internet, once you have set up your ISP account, is the Internet Browser. For Windows this will be Internet Explorer, the version depending on which release of Windows you have on your system.

Windows Vista uses Internet Explorer version 7.0 (IE7). This contains an improved level of security to help defend your system against malicious software. Tabs and quick tabs have been added, to make it easier for you to switch back and forth between websites. Other enhancements include advanced printing, page zooming capabilities, and support for RSS (Really Simple Syndication) feeds (see page 167).

It is the combination of IE7 and Windows Vista that has been used for the illustrations in this book.

Windows XP was initially supplied with IE6 installed.

Upgrade to IE7

Internet Explorer 7 is the recommended choice for secure and convenient Internet access. However, you do not have to upgrade to Windows Vista in order to benefit from IE7. Microsoft has developed a special, stand-alone version of Internet Explorer 7.0 that runs under Windows XP with SP2. What's more, they make it available free of charge.

For instructions on downloading and installing the new version, go to **http://www.microsoft.com/downloads**, and search for **Internet Explorer 7**.

Alternatively, call your local Microsoft office to ask for information. They may have a CD available to save you downloading the software.

Setting Up

Don't forget

Generally, everything you need for accessing the Internet will already have been installed and often pre-configured for you by your computer supplier, so you can go straight on to starting your browser (see page 17).

Hot tip

There's usually a setup CD available from your ISP that will take you step by step through the connection process, with explanations at each stage. This will avoid setting up your connection manually.

In most cases, the instructions you require to set up and configure your Internet connection will be made available by the Internet Service Provider you have selected. However, in Windows Vista the Network Connection Wizard provides guidance for creating the connection. This may be useful when you are setting up, for example, a simple dial-up connection, perhaps using the ISP account from your previous computer.

1. Select Start, type the search term **network** and choose the **Network and Sharing Center**

2. Click the link to **Set up a Connection or Network**

3. Choose your preferred connection option, for example **Dial up**, then click the Next button and enter the phone number, user name and account password

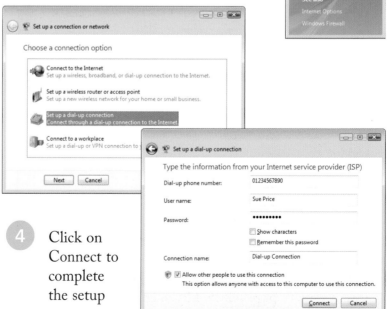

4. Click on Connect to complete the setup

Starting Internet Explorer

The first step in browsing the Internet is to start your Internet browser software (e.g. Internet Explorer). There are two methods that you might use:

1 Click the Start button, and select **Internet Explorer** at the top of the Start menu

2 If you have the **Quick Launch bar** enabled, click its Internet Explorer icon

In either case, the Internet Explorer application will be opened. If it is not already active, your connection to the Internet will be established. When the connection completes, the default web page is displayed.

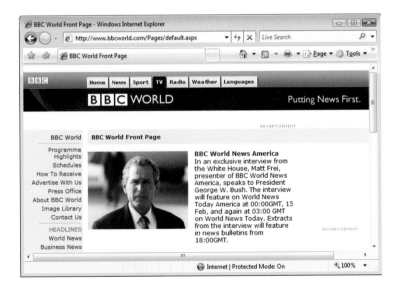

This is known as your Home page, and you'll see the same page each time you start your browser, or whenever you press the Home button on the Command Bar. The page gets defined when your software is installed or re-configured, and is usually a news page selected by your ISP.

Hot tip

To enable the Quick Launch bar, right-click the Taskbar, select Properties and click the Show Quick Launch box, then click OK.

Hot tip

Default means a particular value or setting, in this case a web page, that is assigned automatically, and remains in effect until you cancel or change it.

17

Don't forget

You can change the 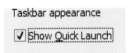 defined home page to a web page that you prefer, or specify several home pages to display at the start. See page 32 for details.

Internet Explorer Window

Your browser is the key component in any Internet activity so you should become familiar with all of its features.

Title bar

Address bar   Tab bar   Toolbar   Search box

Information bar

Favorites Center

Main Window

Status bar   Security Settings   Scroll bars   Zoom

Command buttons

Extra buttons

Hot tip

To add extra buttons or to remove buttons, right-click the Toolbar, and select Customize Command Bar, Add or Remove Commands.

Toolbar buttons

Home
Feeds
Print
Page
Tools
Help

Size
Read Mail
Encoding
Edit
Cut
Copy
Paste
Full Screen

Back
Forward
Recent Pages
Refresh
Stop Loading
Search
Options
Favorites Center
Add Favorites

2 Browse the Internet

The Internet is an enormous library of information, but it is not at all well organized, so you have to locate what you need, by name, through links or by searching, using descriptive keywords, taking full advantage of the capabilities of your browsing software.

Web Page Address

To find your way around the Internet, you need to understand web page addresses. For example, the sample home page (see page 17) has this web address:

> http://www.nytimes.com/index.html

This address is made up of several parts:

- **http://**   Indicates web pages
- **www.nytimes.com**   The web server name
- **index.html**   The web page name

The web server name is itself made up of several parts:

- **www**   Indicates a host computer
- **nytimes**   The company or owner name
- **com**   The type of website

There are a number of other website types that you will encounter. These include:

- **com**   Commercial website
- **org**   Organization – usually non-profit
- **ac**   Academic (e.g. university)
- **gov**   Government department

For all these web types, there are international forms, where an additional section indicates the country, for example:

- **co.uk, org.uk, ac.uk**   United Kingdom
- **com.au, org.au, edu.au**   Australia
- **co.in, org.in, ac.in**   India

Google illustrates the range of international domains supported, via their **Language Tools** link (see page 14).

Don't forget

The web server name incorporates the Domain name, which consists of owner name and website type, in this case nytimes.com. Other examples of domain names are:

    microsoft.com
    elderhostel.org

20

Beware

Individuals as well as companies can register domain names of many different types, so the name itself does not tell you anything about the owner.

Hot tip

Although there are general similarities, the naming is not entirely consistent, country to country. Some countries use co instead of com, and ac instead of edu.

Open a Web Page

If you find a web page address in an article or advertisement, or are given a web address by a friend, you can direct the browser to display that page. For example, to display the web page **www.pagat.com/boston/bridge.html**:

1 Start Internet Explorer (see page 17) if required, and click the address bar area. The address is highlighted

2 Type the required web page address. This replaces the existing highlighted address

3 Press **Enter**, or click the blue arrow button, to display the required page

4 You may see a progress indicator on the Status bar, depending on how quickly the web page loads

Links

Don't forget

Hyperlinks are the fundamental element in the World Wide Web. They are also used in electronic documents such as Adobe's PDF files.

When you've displayed one web page, you can usually go on to another page without having to type a web page address. Instead, you click on items on the current page that have web addresses associated with them. These items are called Links (or Hyperlinks). They are often descriptive text, underlined and colored blue, for example.

To confirm whether a part of the page is a link:

1 Place the mouse pointer over the item. If it is a link, the pointer changes to a hand symbol, to indicate that there is a link address

2 The target location is shown on the status bar

Hot tip

Sometimes, the text or graphic will change color when the mouse pointer moves over it, or it will flash, to draw your attention to the associated link.

3 Sometimes, the link will be a graphic image with no distinguishing marks. Again, the mouse pointer changes to a hand symbol, to indicate a link

4 Often, the graphic image will have a **Tool Tip** description, which appears when you place the mouse pointer over the image

22

Follow Links

To follow a link, left-click the associated text or graphic.

Alphabetical Index

1 Click the Alphabetical Index link (see page 21).
This leads to a page with links A to Z, defining
sections on the same page, organized alphabetically

2 Click the **H** link to move down the page to the
location **www.pagat.com/alpha.html#h**

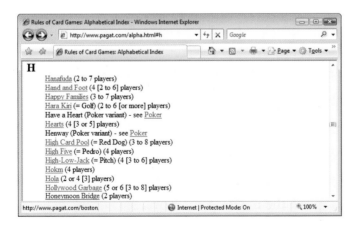

When you visit a location the color **Honeymoon Bridge**
of the link changes, typically from blue to purple, providing
a visual cue that you have followed that particular link.

Address Help

Internet Explorer offers you help with entering web page addresses, in several ways.

1 Click the arrow at the end of the Address bar, to see a list of web page addresses that you have typed previously, and click the one that you want

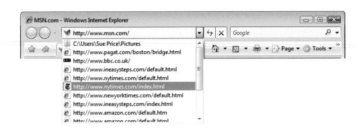

2 If you start typing an address (as on page 20), Internet Explorer lists previously visited web pages that match the part entered so far. As soon as you see the required web page, click the entry to open it

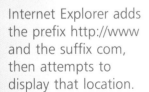

3 Type the company or organization name on the address bar, and then press Ctrl+Enter

Add to Favorites

When you visit a web page that you find useful, make it easy to find another time by adding it to your list of favorites.

1 While viewing the web page, click the Add to Favorites button and select **Add to Favorites**

2 The title of the page is suggested as the name, or you can type another perhaps more descriptive name. Click **Add** to put the page details onto the main list

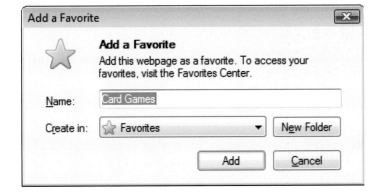

3 Click on the **Favorites Center** button to display the list, and select any page you wish to visit

Hot tip

Pages you visit every day can become your home pages, so they open whenever Internet Explorer opens. See page 32.

Don't forget

Press the New Folders button to create a subfolder in the Favorites list. Click the down-arrow to select a subfolder in which to store the web page details.

Hot tip

If you forgot to add a web page and you want to find it again, click the History tab in the Favorites Center, and you'll see the pages you have visited over the recent period of time.

Searching

If you have no idea of the correct website, Internet Explorer will carry out a search on your behalf.

1 Click in the **Search** box to the right of the Address bar, type some keywords appropriate to the website you want, and press Enter

2 Internet Explorer uses your default search engine to find web pages that are related to your search terms

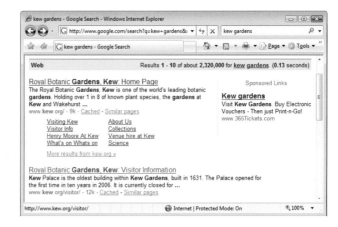

3 Scroll down or page forward as required until you find the website you want, then click the header

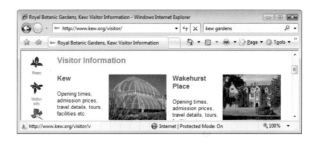

4 Press the **Back** button to return to the search results

Add Search Providers

If you prefer to use a different search provider, you can make additional providers available, and change the default.

1 Click the down arrow next to the search box, and select **Find More Providers**, to open the Windows Search Guide at Microsoft's website

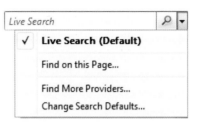

Hot tip

You can also search straight from the Address bar. Type Find or Go followed by the search words, to display the results in the current window.

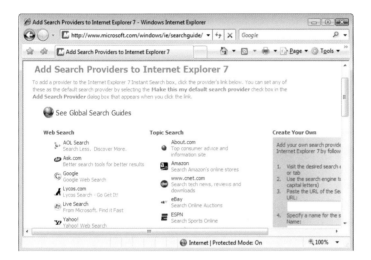

2 Click the hyperlink for your preferred search provider, to display the **Add Provider** dialog

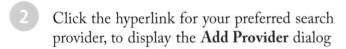

3 Click in the box to **Make this my default search provider**, and then press **Add Provider**

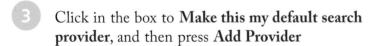

4 Select any other provider that you want to add (this time without clicking the box)

Don't forget

Click an entry on the list to make it your choice for the current session.

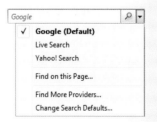

Specific Searches

The normal search is for pages across the Web, but there are alternatives such as local pages, groups, news, or images.

1 Type your keywords into the search box, and search using Google, to list the matching web pages

2 Click **Images** to repeat the search, this time locating relevant images, which are displayed as thumbnails

3 Click the down arrow next to **All Image Sizes** to limit the images selected to small, medium or large sizes

Using Tabs

Tabs allow you to have more than one website open at the same time, without having to use separate windows. With web pages, links and search results on separate tabs, you switch between them using Quick Tabs. To open a new tab:

1 Click the **New Tab** button on the tab row or press Ctrl+T, to open a new blank page

2 You will see the Welcome to Tabbed Browsing page and the **Quick Tabs** button is displayed

3 Click the **Don't show this page again** box at the bottom of the page to get a blank page in future

☑ Don't show this page again

4 Type the web page location on the address bar, and the specified web page opens on the new tab

Don't forget

In previous versions of Internet Explorer, you need to open an additional copy of Internet Explorer, or right-click a hyperlink and select Open in new window, to have more than one web page open at the same time.

Hot tip

The Welcome to Tabbed Browsing page lists the benefits and provides some advice for getting started with tabs.

Hot tip

The title for each page appears on the appropriate tab, while the title for the currently selected tab appears on the Internet Explorer titlebar.

Open New Tab

Hot tip

There are several ways for you to specify a web page address, and have it open it on a new tab, as in steps 1, 2 or 3.

1 Type the web page location on the address bar, with the current tab displayed, then press **Alt+Enter**

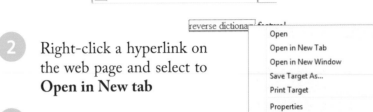

2 Right-click a hyperlink on the web page and select to **Open in New tab**

Hot tip

If you have a three button mouse, select the hyperlink with the middle button. When you have a wheel on your mouse, that also acts as a middle button. In either case, the page opens on a new tab.

3 Hold down the **Ctrl** key as you left-click a hyperlink on the web page

4 Click the **Quick Tabs** button to review all the tabbed pages, and select one you want

Hot tip

Click the Tab List button next to Quick Tabs, to select from a list, or click the Scroll buttons to find a particular page on the tab row.

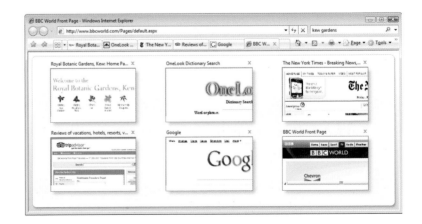

Close Tabs

Having opened a number of tabs, you can close them individually or as a group.

1 Click the [X] on an individual tab to close it, or select the tab with the center mouse button

2 Right-click a tab or one of the Quick Tabs thumbnails, and select to close just that tab, or to close all the other tabs (leaving that tab open)

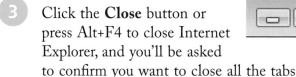

3 Click the **Close** button or press Alt+F4 to close Internet Explorer, and you'll be asked to confirm you want to close all the tabs

4 Click the **Show Options** button and you will be offered the opportunity to **Open these the next time I use Internet Explorer**

5 It's best to leave **Do not show me this dialog again** unchecked as this dialog does serve a useful purpose

Don't forget

You can also close the current tab by pressing Ctrl+W. To close all the tabs except the current tab, press Ctrl+Alt+W.

31

Hot tip

To save a group of tabs and make them available for reload, click the Add to Favorites button (see page 25) and select Add Tab Group to Favorites. You will need to provide a folder name.

Change Home Page

You can change the web page used as the initial page when Internet Explorer starts up.

1. Open the preferred web page by typing its location on the address bar (see page 20)

2. Click the down arrow next to the Home Page button

3. To use the current web page, select the option to Change Home Page

4. Select the option to **Use this webpage as your only home page**, then click Yes to apply the change

The specified page opens automatically, when you click the Home button, or whenever you start Internet Explorer.

Blank Home Page

If you decide that you do not require a home page at all:

1. Select Remove, Remove All, and Internet Explorer will simply start on a blank page

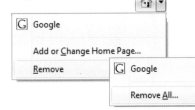

3 Puzzles and Solutions

Use online reference materials to look up words, get solutions to crossword clues, locate facts or resolve anagrams. You can also use the Internet as a source of entertaining puzzles and quizzes, or to locate online books, especially the classics, which you can read and research.

Solve Crosswords

You might make a start by using the Internet to help you with a crossword. Suppose you have a partially solved crossword and want to use the Internet to help complete it.

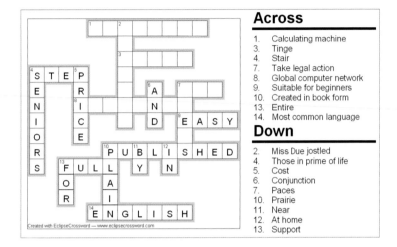

Across

1. Calculating machine
3. Tinge
4. Stair
7. Take legal action
8. Global computer network
9. Suitable for beginners
10. Created in book form
13. Entire
14. Most common language

Down

2. Miss Due jostled
4. Those in prime of life
5. Cost
6. Conjunction
7. Paces
10. Prairie
11. Near
12. At home
13. Support

1. Type the keywords **solve crossword** in the Search box and click the Search button

2. The website at **www.oneacross.com** offers free help with crosswords (and anagrams and cryptograms)

Resolve Clues

The OneAcross website allows you to enter complete clues, along with the number of letters required. For example:

1 Type the clue **Take legal action** and the pattern **???** (meaning three letters, all unknown), and click Go!

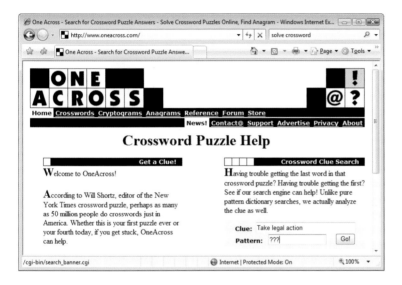

2 The website displays the answers that it finds, with the most likely answer shown first

Hot tip

Solve clue 7 across: Take legal action (3)

Don't forget

When you think you know one or more letters, replace the ?s in the appropriate positions by the expected letter. Use upper case if you are sure you have the correct letter, lower case otherwise.

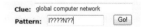

Find Anagrams

Many crosswords incorporate anagrams in the clues. The anagram server at **www.wordsmith.org** helps with these.

1 Type the anagram word or words, leaving out spaces, e.g. **miss due** and click **Get Anagrams**

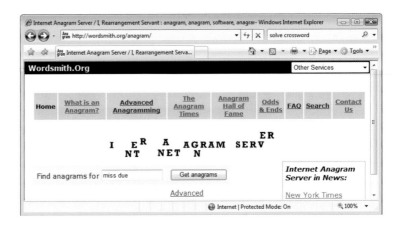

2 The website displays all the answers that it can find. These can include multiple words, abbreviations, acronyms etc

3 For more specific answers, use the Advanced Anagramming option

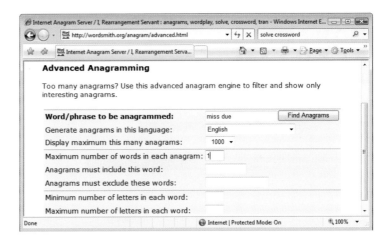

Look Up Words

You can look up words in an online dictionary, for example:

1 Visit **www.onelook.com**, and type the pattern for the word, using **???**s and inserting letters you know

2 OneLook defaults to **All Matches**, and lists the potential answers in alphabetic order

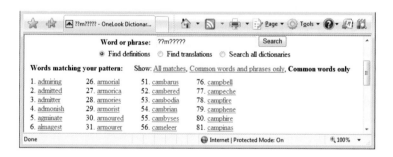

3 Add words from the clue (separated by a colon from the word pattern). The most likely will be listed first

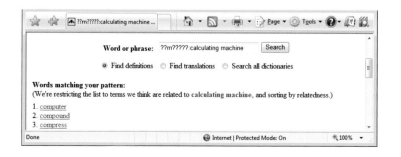

Hot tip

Solve clue 1 across: Calculating machine(8)

Don't forget

The OneLook Dictionaries website has indexed about eight million words, from around 1000 dictionaries. It finds word patterns and definitions.

Hot tip

If there are many possibilities, only the first 100 are listed. Try selecting Common Words Only, to reduce the number.

Beware

Words from the clue may not help if you are completing a cryptic crossword, since they may not appear in the literal definitions.

Crosswords Online

The Internet doesn't just help you solve crosswords, it is also a rich source of crosswords. You will soon find your own favorite sites, but to help get you started, try one of the newspapers. For example:

 Type **www.washingtonpost.com/crosswords** on the address bar and press Enter to open the web page

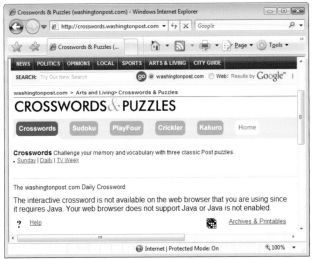

 Click the Archives and Printables link, select a date and click the Printable Puzzle link

 You must print out the crossword and its clues to complete the puzzle

February 15, 2008 - "SAT Exam"
By Randolph Ross

ACROSS
1. Word of warning
7. Summer coolers
11. Gift topper
14. Heartthrob's fan
15. Romance writer Roberts
16. "___ Lazy River"
17. Steak-lobster combo, on some menus
19. Square dance partner
20. Summer coolers, for short
21. 18th Pres.
22. Figure on ice
24. Didn't react to
28. Kind of fit
30. Fed up
34. New York city where Mark Twain is buried
37. Order to a broker
38. Team
39. 24 horas
40. Authorize
43. Source of evidence
44. Village People hit
46. TV room
72. On one's ___ (alert)

@2008 Randolph Ross. Distributed by

Interactive Crosswords

You can complete crosswords interactively, but you may need to install or activate Java software support first.

1 Click **More Info** to get details of Java support

2 Windows Vista Help explains how to enable Java in Internet Explorer

Beware

If you do not already have Java installed, you'll need to visit www.java.com to download the free software.

3 Select **Play Crosswords** to begin playing an interactive puzzle

4 Select a square, click the Across or Down clue and type the letters for your answer, using the **Check** or **Save** icons as needed

Archive

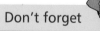
Save

Check

Don't forget

If all else fails, click the Reveal icon to show the selected letter or word, or to display the whole solution. Click the Archive icon to view further puzzles.

Sudoku

If you want a change from crosswords, you might switch to Sudoku. The Internet will provide advice and suggestions for completing the puzzles you find in magazines, and offer puzzles for you to play online or print out to complete later.

Hot tip

In Sudoku (Number Place) digits 1 to 9 are added to a partially completed 9×9 grid, such that all the rows, columns and 3x3 regions contain one instance of every digit from 1 to 9.

Hot tip

Click Select a puzzle, and specify the level, then go to a puzzle at random, or enter the specific number to repeat a previous puzzle.

Level: Easy ▼
Number: 3546747876
Go to this puzzle

Don't forget

Click Options to set the timer, to change the strictness of the progress report, or to allow you to "pencil in" multiple possibilities in a cell.

1   Go to **www.websudoku.com** which claims to have billions of Sudoku puzzles for you to play

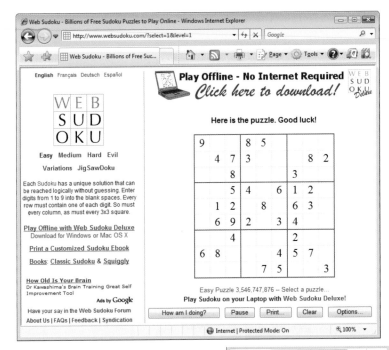

2   Click an empty cell and type a suitable digit, based on the contents of other cells. Your entries are shown in blue italics

3   To check your progress, click **How am I doing?** You'll be warned if you've entered a wrong number

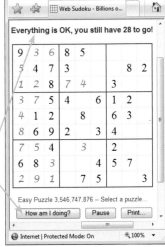

Solving Puzzles

Here are some useful websites that explain some of the techniques involved in solving Sudoku puzzles.

1 At **www.simetric.co.uk/sudoku** you'll find three tutorials that demonstrate solving Sudoku puzzles

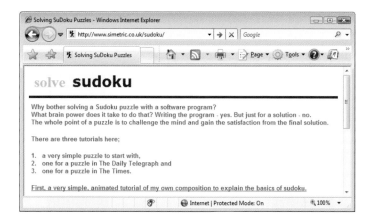

Hot tip

The tutorials start with a simple, animated example and go step by step through the solving of actual Sudoku puzzles, to illustrate some of the techniques that you can use.

2 There's a comprehensive guide to solving Sudoku, at **www.sudoku.org.uk/PDF/Solving_Sudoku.pdf**

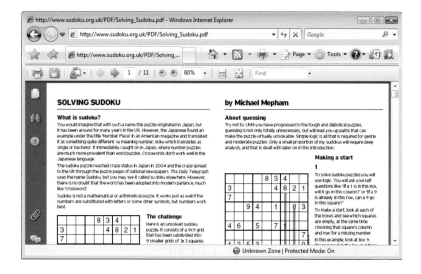

Don't forget

This report tells us there is a total of 3546146300288 valid Sudoku grids, after making allowance for symmetrical repeats.

3 Finally, for the count of valid Sudoku grids, see **www.afjarvis.staff.shef.ac.uk/sudoku/sudoku.pdf**

Brain Aerobics

Brain teasers, quizzes and games are not just for fun or to pass the time, they also provide essential mental exercise.

1 Search for **brain teasers for seniors** to find sites such as **www.clevelandseniors.com/forever/mindex.htm**

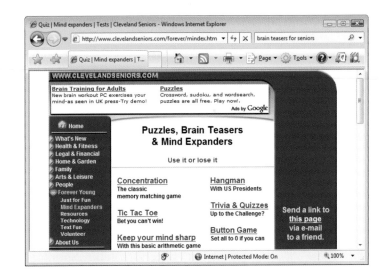

2 Select one of the 15 or so links of Mind Expanders, for example Concentration or Trivia & Quizzes

3 If you want more cerebral exercise, visit website **www.mensa.org** and click **Mensa Workout**

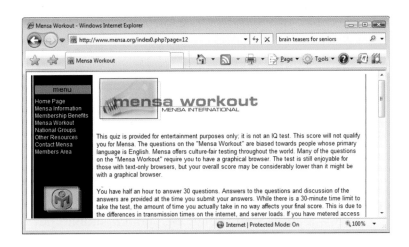

Web Encyclopedia

To help you answer all the quizzes you find, you'll need good reference material. Make a start with the Web encyclopedia that you can edit and update, as well as reference.

1 Go to **www.wikipedia.org** and choose your preferred language, e.g. English

English
The Free Encyclopedia
2 218 000+ articles
Français
L'encyclopédie libre
619 000+ articles
Deutsch
Die freie Enzyklopädie
705 000+ Artikel

2 Select the Main Page, and scroll down to see the list of sister projects, also user-maintained

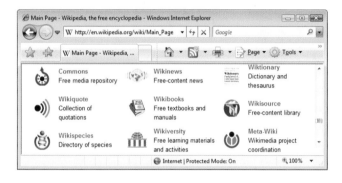

3 Click **Sign in / Create Account** to specify your user name, password and (optionally) your email address

4 Explore the articles. Search for topics, or just click the Random Article link to see what appears

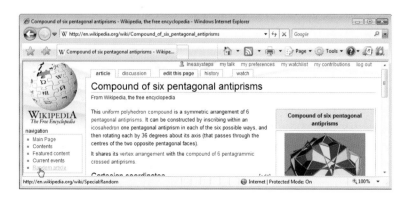

Don't forget

Wikipedia is hosted by the Wikimedia Foundation, a non-profit organization that also hosts a range of other projects.

Beware

In principle anybody can contribute to Wikipedia. In practice, older articles tend to be more comprehensive and balanced, while newer articles may contain misinformation or unencyclopedic info, or even vandalism.

43

Don't forget

It isn't essential to create an account, but it does let you communicate with other Wikipedia users.

Internet Public Library

The Internet Public Library (IPL), managed and maintained by the University of Michigan School of Information, offers library services to Internet users, helping them to find, evaluate and organize information resources.

Hot tip

The IPL provides an annotated collection of high quality internet resources, selected by the IPL staff as providing accurate and factual information.

1 Visit **www.ipl.org** to see subject collections, ready reference and reading room material, etc.

Don't forget

To change the screen resolution, right-click the desktop, select Personalize and Display Settings, and drag the Resolution slider.

2 There's so much information, a high screen resolution may be useful. This example is 1280 x 1024, but this makes the text rather small

3 Click the Zoom button at the foot of the window, to switch between 100%, 125%, and 150%, and so enlarge the view

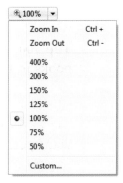

4 Click the down-arrow to choose a preset level between 50% and 400%, or choose Custom and set an exact level (10% - 1000%)

Online Classics

You can find the full text for many thousands of books on the Internet, in an electronic (ebook) format that is ideal for searching for particular details. They are books whose copyright has expired, and in the main they are classics. There are online books on Wikipedia and on IPL, but perhaps the best source for free ebooks is Project Gutenberg.

1. Type **www.gutenberg.org** and press Enter to display the home page for the website

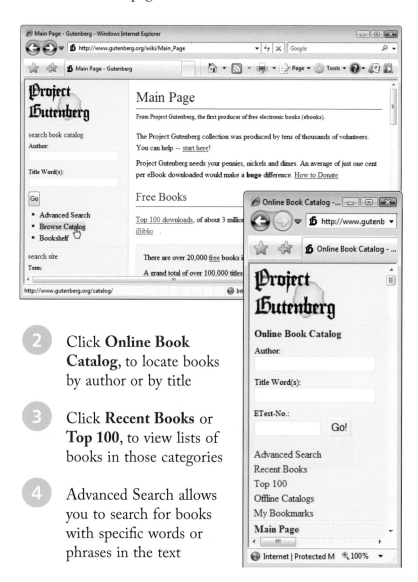

2. Click **Online Book Catalog**, to locate books by author or by title

3. Click **Recent Books** or **Top 100**, to view lists of books in those categories

4. Advanced Search allows you to search for books with specific words or phrases in the text

Hot tip

You can participate in Project Gutenberg, for example by volunteering to proof read individual pages of books.

Beware

If you don't live in the US, you should check the copyright laws in your country before downloading an ebook.

Don't forget

You can also browse the database, by author or by title, arranged alphabetically.

Online Reference

When it's reference books you want, visit the Bartleby website, where you can access a wide range of well known books.

1 Go to **www.bartleby.com** and click the down-arrow next to the Search box to choose the specific type

2 You can search the whole site, or a specific section (reference, verse, fiction, or non-fiction), or just a specific book in a section

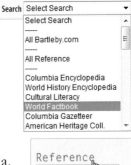

3 To search in a subsection of the references, click the Reference link and then select Encyclopedia,

Dictionary, Thesaurus, Quotations or English Usage, each of which includes several references

4 Chess and Bridge

Even if you are home alone, you can participate in games of chess or of bridge over the Internet. You can play against the computer or against human opponents. You can watch others play, historical games or live events. You'll also get lots of help on the Internet to improve your game.

Chess Games

Chessgames.com is an online database of historic chess games that help chess players to develop their games.

1 To find a game, go to **www.chessgames.com** to display the home page, with several search options

2 Type a plain text game description in the search box, for example the player names, and the year, the result or the opening move

3 Alternatively, fill in the fields on the Advanced Search form:

- Year
- Player
- White or Black
- Opposing player
- No. of moves
- Opening (name)
- ECO code
- Result

4 Click the **Find Chess Games** button. The matching games will be listed. Click the game you want to see

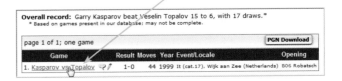

Overall record: Garry Kasparov beat Veselin Topalov 15 to 6, with 17 draws.*
* Based on games present in our database; may not be complete.

Game		Result	Moves	Year	Event/Locale		Opening
1. Kasparov vs Topalov		1-0	44	1999	It (cat.17), Wijk aan Zee (Netherlands)		B06 Robatsch

page 1 of 1; one game   PGN Download

View Game

A chess board will be displayed, along with the list of moves that make up that particular game.

Beware

You'll need the Java software enabled (see page 39), and you may have to switch Java Viewers to find the one that works best on your system.

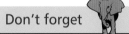

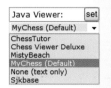

Don't forget

Click anywhere in the table, to view the state of play at that stage.

1. Click the arrows to step forward or backward through the game, one move at a time

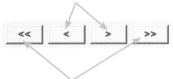

2. Click one of the double arrows, to move to the start point or to the end point of the game

3. Click the Guess the Move box to run the chess training and take the part of a player

Hot tip

The games are stored using PGN (Portable Game Notation), a simple text format which you can download and import to Chess software running on your PC.

Play Computer

Studying chess games is educational, but you really need to play games in order to improve your skill level. There are many websites where you can play other people, friends or strangers, but perhaps you could start off playing against a computer program, such as Little Chess Partner.

1. Go to **www.chessica.de/gamezone.html** and click the first Play button, to play against the computer

50

2. Click the board to start, then drag to move a (white) chess piece turn by turn. The computer won't let you make an illegal move

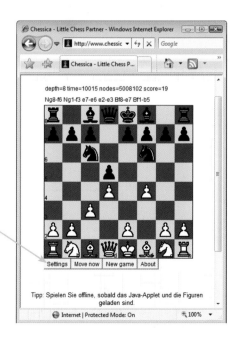

3. Click the **Settings** button to change the thinking time or the depth of analysis used by the computer

If you find the Little Chess Partner too challenging, there's an easier program that you can play against, to get practise.

1 Scroll down and click the link **Try This!** which appears below the chess board display (see page 50)

(see page 50)

2 Choose Black or White for the computer, and then take your turns – select a piece (which changes to **purple**) then click the destination to make your moves. Only legal moves are allowed

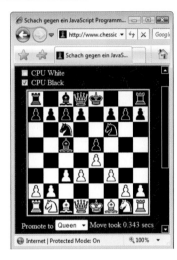

3 The Game Log records all the moves made

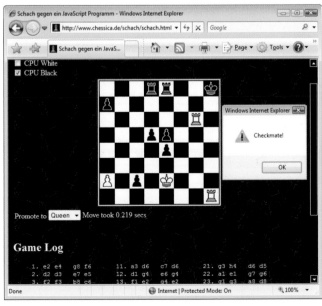

51

Chess Server

Hot tip

On FICS, you can find casual games, or play serious chess, with other (human) players or with a strong computer.

To introduce yourself to the world of chess on the Internet:

1   Visit the Free Internet Chess Server (FICS) at **www.freechess.org** to register for playing online

Don't forget

FICS caters for all levels of player – from the very beginner, to the grand master.

Hot tip

The available interfaces for Windows Vista are listed. The table shows how many connections have been recorded on FICS with each of the 3 most used interfaces. This is merely indicative, as the newer interfaces will of course have fewer connections.

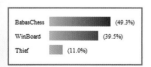

2   Click the **Downloads** link to look for a graphical interface, the easiest way to connect to FICS

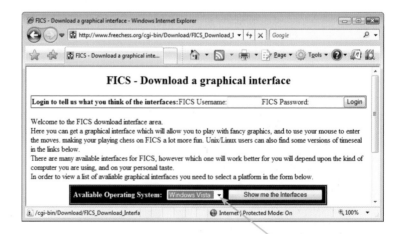

3   Select your operating system (e.g. Windows Vista) and click the button **Show me the Interfaces**

4   Click the URL for the one you want to try out

Graphical Interface

You can download Winboard to your computer, from Tim Mann's chess pages at **www.tim-mann.org/xboard.html**

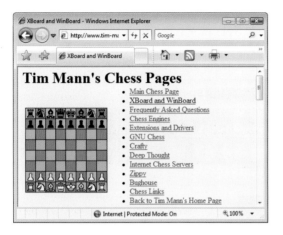

1 Click the **XBoard and WinBoard** link and scroll down for the download link and other details

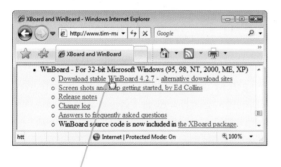

2 Click the **Download** link and select Save to add winboard-4_2_7b.exe to your downloads folder. Double-click this file to install WinBoard

3 The WinBoard folder on the Start menu has an entry for Freechess.org, the FICS server, plus various other chess servers and games

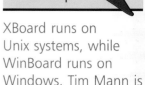

Visit Server

You can visit the club as a guest, to help you decide if you'd like to become a full member.

1 Select Start, All Programs, WinBoard, and click the **Chess Server – freechess.org** entry

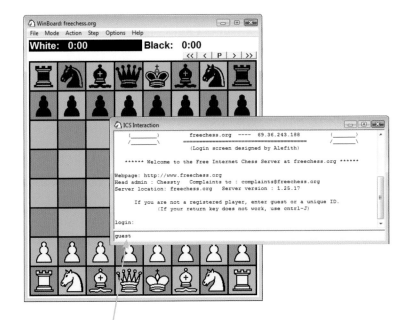

2 Type **guest** and press Enter. FICS will give you a unique ID, in this case **GuestYHMW**

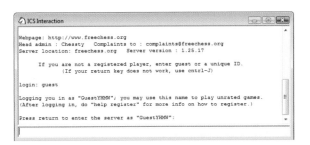

3 Soon you'll start receiving copies of messages from other guests or registered members, seeking opponents to play. Type **play nn** (where nn is the game number specified) to respond

Observe Games

You may send a message to see if games are being relayed.

1 Type **tell relay listgames** and press Enter

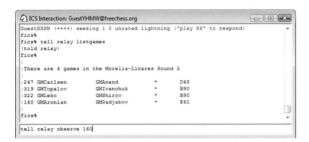

2 Type **tell relay observe 160** to view that game

3 The WinBoard displays the current position for the selected game, then continues to display all the moves as the game proceeds

4 Type **help intro_basics** for a list of basic commands, and type **help intro_welcome** for additional details, or type **Exit** to terminate your session

Hot tip

If you get the response "There are no games in progress", try again later, or watch out for announcements from Relay.

55

Don't forget

Other useful files include:
   intro_general
   intro_information
   intro_moving
   intro_playing
   register

Great Bridge Links

If bridge is your game, it is well supported on the Internet. There's an organized list of bridge-related websites at the nicely named Great Bridge Links.

 Visit the website **www.greatbridgelinks.com**. The main sets of links are listed at the top of the screen

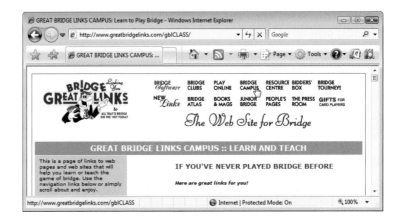

 Click **Bridge Campus** for links to web pages and websites that will help you learn (or teach) the game of bridge. If you are new to bridge, there's a lesson for complete beginners at Richard Pavlicek's teaching site **www.rpbridge.net/1a00.htm**

If you already play bridge, you might want to visit one of the more comprehensive sites listed, for example:

1 Visit Karen Walker's Bridge Library at website **www.prairienet.org/bridge** to investigate her collection of class handouts and reference sheets

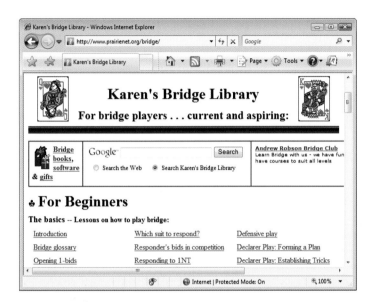

2 The American Contract Bridge League has a home page at **www.acbl.org/**, with information and news

3 The links at the Canadian Bridge Federation website **www.cbf.ca** include one that's specifically for Seniors

Online Bridge Clubs

When you are ready to play Bridge online, you'll find numerous websites to help you get started and find partners.

1 On Great Bridge Links, click **Play Online** for a list of online Bridge clubs, where individuals can play bridge against others from around the world, of all levels and experience

2 Click the **Go** button next to an online club, for example **Bridge Base Online**, to display details of the club

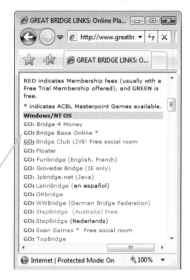

3 Information including contact details will be displayed. Click the website address provided, to visit the club

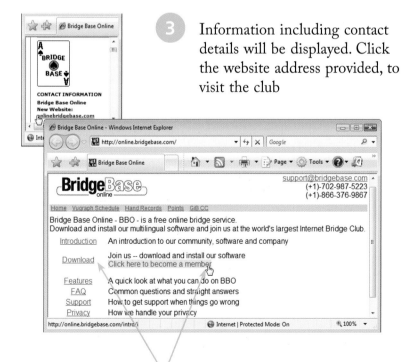

4 Click either **Download** or **Click here to become a member**, to begin the procedure to join the club

Download Software

To join Bridge Base Online (BBO) you need to download and install the associated software on your PC.

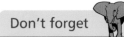

Don't forget

You can choose to Save the file to your hard disk then double-click the downloaded file to run the program later. See page 147.

① Select an option to download the file. There are several methods proposed, in case of problems

② Click **Run** to download and install the software

Beware

You may get a security warning that the publisher could not be verified. If you have any doubts, select Don't Run, then Save the file as noted above and scan for viruses before installing.

③ Follow the prompts, and accept default location and settings

④ Double click the desktop shortcut, or select the Start menu entries **Bridge Base Inc**, **Bridge Base Online** to view Bridge movies (see page 60) or to register and log (see page 61)

59

Hot tip

You cannot play bridge at Bridge Base Online directly from the website – you must log in using the downloaded software.

Bridge Movies

A Bridge Movie is an interactive presentation, based on a bridge book, article, quiz or match. To view a movie:

1 Click **Open Bridge Movie from your computer** (see page 59), pick an entry from the folder, and click the Open button

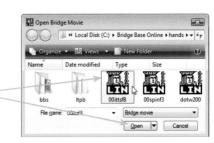

2 Click an entry to display the deal and the bidding

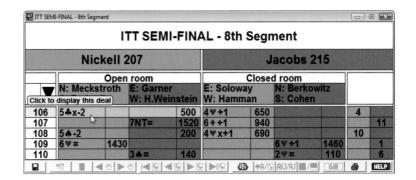

3 Click the **Next Page** button to step through the hand. Select Next Board to review more deals

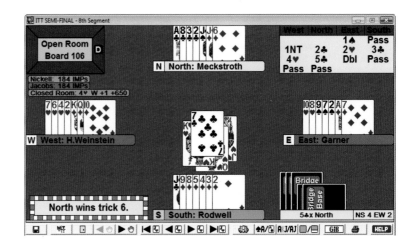

Log in to BBO

1 If you have previously registered, enter your user name and password and click **Log in** to start

2 If you are a new member, click **Register**

3 Provide a user name and password, and add the details you wish to record, then click OK

4 When you have logged in, you are allowed into the lobby, from where you can play and improve your bridge

Bridge Base Online - Version 5.0.3

Bridge Base Online — Women's Bridge Festival on line
April 7th - 13th 2008

Click to Play or Watch Bridge!	lneasystep	georgi
	ACBL	Gerardo
Help me find a game!	arigun ☆	macaw
	babela	Walddk ☆
Other Bridge Activities	FFBBO	
Vugraph (live broadcasts with commentary)	In order to choose which members appear in this area, click "Options" below then "Select members to display".	
ACBL Masterpoint Tournaments		
Edit Your Profile and User Options	Members in this color are here to help you. Left click to send a private chat message.	
Buy BB$ -- used for ACBL entry fees, renting robots, etc.	Members in this color are your friends. Right click to define a member as your friend.	
Our Online Store		
Useful Links and Information		
Masterpoint Races	Options	12533 Players / 9 Displayed

BACK | TABLE | REDEAL | CONV | UNDO | CLAIM | CHAT | ← | → | ↔ | ❀ | ♠A/♣ | ■/▬ | GIB | MOVIE | HELP

Hot tip

You'll be told if your user name is already in use, so you can offer a new one.

Don't forget

Values for your real name, your email address, and your country are required (many members leave them as the default Private). Your skill level and Other information are optional and can be added later.

61

Beware

The details you provide will be visible to all members, so provide limited details until you are sure you want to remain a member.

Kibitz a Table

You can join a table as an observer and watch the game. This is referred to as kibitzing.

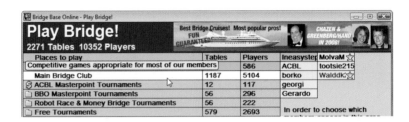

1 Click the **Play Bridge** button, and then enter the main bridge club (as recommended for new users).

Hot tip

If you don't feel ready to jump right in and join a table as a player, start by watching existing games.

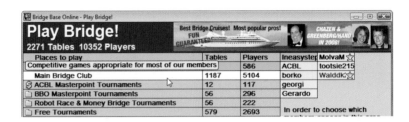

2 The first time you kibitz, find a table that already has several kibitzers, and that doesn't require permission

Don't forget

The padlock symbol means permission is required, either to play at the table or to watch the game (kibitz).

🔒 Permission required to play or kibitz.

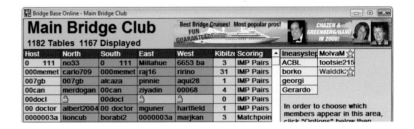

3 You view the game as a bridge movie (see page 60). Press Back to leave the table

Beware

You must observe the proper etiquette. For example, kibitzers may be prohibited from chatting with the players at a table (even when no permission is needed to watch).

Kibitzers cannot chat with players.

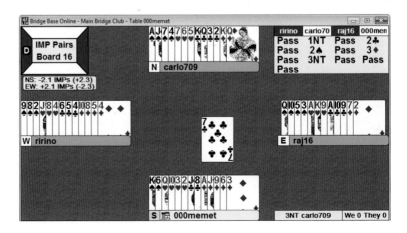

5 Internet Entertainment

Use the Internet as your TV and Radio guide to regular channels or web broadcasts. Check what movies are being released, and what shows are on stage around the world. Or just relax to the sound of classical music.

What's on TV?

Every country has its national and regional television stations, along with numerous local stations. The Internet can help you keep track of them, and even look in on them, since many offer websites and broadcast over the Internet.

64

1 Start with a visit to a TV Station directory such as **wwitv.com** which lists live and on-demand TV broadcasts from around the world

2 Scroll down and select a location, the UK for example, to list all the TV stations available

③ Choose a website to visit the channel's homepage for information about programmes recorded, available to view and scheduled

④ Click a streamed link to view both recorded and live television

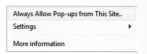

⑤ Windows will need to open a player. A green link will require Windows Media Player and a blue link RealPlayer

Regular TV

Even if you want to watch regular TV (satellite, cable or antenna), the Internet proves useful for searching schedules.

1 TV Zap has links to worldwide television schedules and guides, at the **www.tvzap.com** website

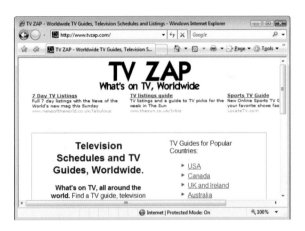

2 Select the country or region you are interested in, e.g. Canada, to list the relevant guides and schedules

3 Choose one of the TV Schedule websites, specify the time period, category and keywords, then follow the prompts to see the schedule for your location

What's on Radio?

You can find out what's on terrestrial radio stations, and listen to radio stations that broadcast over the Internet.

1 Type the web address **radiostationworld.com** in the browser address bar

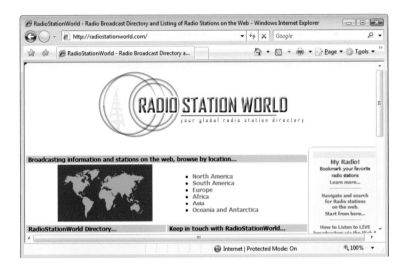

Hot tip

The original address for this website was TVRadioWorld.com and this will still display the site. However, the emphasis has now switched to radio broadcasts.

67

2 Click the link **Navigate** and search for radio stations, select the location from the table and then click Go

> Navigate and search for Radio stations on the web. Start from here...

Don't forget

As with TV over the Internet (see page 65) you'll need a player to listen to the broadcast programs.

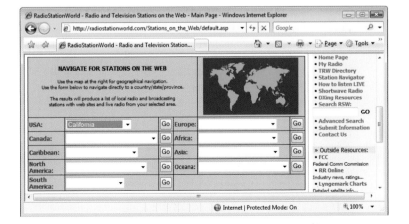

Internet Radio

The towns and regions in the selected state or country are listed, with links to the lists of their local radio stations (with the number of stations shown after the link, e.g. [#81]).

1 Click the Radio stations link to list all the radio stations for the area

2 Click the Webcasters link to select only those stations that broadcast over the Internet

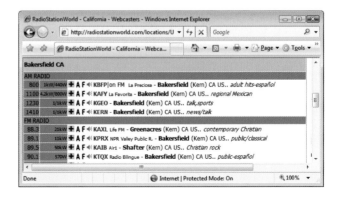

68

3 Each station has its type of content and, where necessary, its language identified

4 Click the speaker symbol for a particular station to select it and listen live

5 You will be transferred to a window that identifies the media player required to play the radio stream

---

You are about to listen to:
KRTH
from Los Angeles, CA

Click here to receive webcast.
Note: This webcast utilizes WinAmp (.pls), but can also be heard using several other media players

---

6 For some radio stations you may have to visit the station website to start the broadcast

7 Click the link to receive the webcast. The required media player will be installed or initialized and the radio station should begin playing

Hot tip

Click the [+] button to add the station to your My Radio list, a sort of favorites list maintained for you by Radio Station World.

Don't forget

Normally, the stations will support one or more of the same media players used for TV broadcasts (see page 65).

Beware

Note that Radio Station World warns that some US radio stations may be blocked if you are listening outside the United States.

Visit the BBC

You can visit particular broadcasters, such as CNN, NBC or the BBC, to see what features they have to offer.

The UK version covers UK related news, sport and weather and UK radio and TV. The International version covers world news, sport and weather along with the BBC's international radio and TV services. You can reselect your default version at any time.

1 Visit the BBC website at **www.bbc.co.uk** and select the UK version or the International version as appropriate to you

2 Click the Radio tab to see the stations and programs available, and to listen in to broadcasts

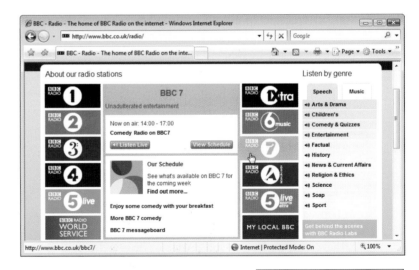

Don't forget

The Listen Again sections on the BBC website allow you to catch up with programs that you missed the first time around.

3 Hover over a channel and click Listen Live, or choose a genre to view a list of recorded programmes and Listen Again

Hollywood Movies

Maybe movies are your preference. As you'd expect, the
Internet has lots to say about them. For many people, the
home of movies is in Hollywood, California.

1 You'll find a comprehensive list of Hollywood movies
at the **www.hollywood.com** website

Don't forget

As usual, you can
right-click the link and
select Open Link in
New Tab, rather than a
separate window.

2 Scroll down and click the **Movie Calendar** link to
see what movies are planned for future months

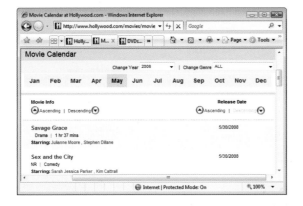

Hot tip

Click the month to list
movies for that period,
and click the movie
title for details and
reviews.

3 If your interest is in Indian
and Asian movies, visit the
alternative movie website at
www.bollywoodworld.com

New York Theater

Hot tip

Normally, in the USA we write "theater", while in the UK it's "theatre". However, most American theater companies adopt the "re" ending for their names, even if the buildings are still referred to as theaters. Likewise, you will find details of the New York shows at www.nytheatre.com

Beware

There is a website at www.nytheater.com dealing more with sporting events and concerts than theater.

nyTheater.com

Don't forget

Starred shows are considered by the site editor to be noteworthy or of special interest.

☆ **The Crucible**
Echo Lake (starts Mar 6)

If all the world's a stage for you, visit the theater websites to see what shows are on.

1 For New York City theater information, including show listings, look at **www.nytheatre.com**

2 Click the **Venue Listings** link to list all theaters with the address and current/future shows

MORE LISTINGS:
   Coming Attractions
   Festival Calendar
   One Night Only
   Venue Listings

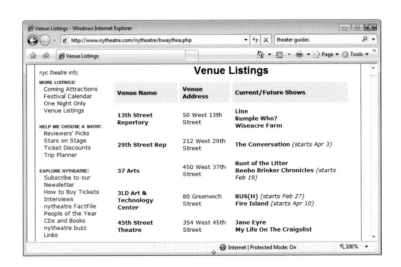

3 Click the underlined theater name to find out more about that venue, including details such as exact location, travel directions and the seating plan. Click the show title to find out more about the show itself

London Theater Guide

If you are planning to be in London, you can check what's on in the West End at the Official London Theatre site.

1 The **www.officiallondontheatre.co.uk** website has theater news, show lists, ticket purchase, awards etc

2 Click **Theatreland Map** and select the **GIF** link to view the map as an image in the browser

3 Select the **PDF** link to download a higher resolution map and view or print it with Adobe Reader in IE7

Hot tip

If the map is displayed reduced size, to fit in the browser window, click with the Expand Image cursor to see it full size.

Don't forget

If Internet Explorer offers to download the file, you do not have the Adobe Reader installed. See page 74 to add this to your system.

Install Adobe Reader

Adobe Reader may be installed (at no cost) from Adobe's website.

1 Visit **www.adobe.com** and click the button labeled Get Adobe reader

2 Click the **Download now** button for the latest version of Adobe Reader, and follow the prompts

3 Adobe Reader is installed, and Internet Explorer is reconfigured to use Adobe Reader for PDF files

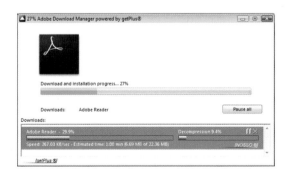

4 When you click on a link to an online PDF document, it will now open in Internet Explorer

Classical Music Archives

If you'd simply like to relax to the sound of classical music, the Internet will not disappoint you.

1 Visit **www.classicalarchives.com** to find a collection of music that you can listen to – without charge

2 Click **Please Read This**, then scroll down to the **Register here** link

3 To register, you provide your name, email address, password, location and phone number

Hot tip

Registered Free Members can play up to five pieces per day. For an annual fee of $25, subscribers are allowed up to 100 plays a day.

Don't forget

There are several links for paid subscribers, but free registration is buried in the details of the Introduction.

Hot tip

The online music is in Windows Media Player format, but subscribers can also save files in MP3 format.

...cont'd

4 When you've completed the form, click the **Free Member Registration** button to submit your details

5 An email is sent to the address you specify. Click the web link provided in the email, to activate membership

6 Click the link to **Return to the Archives' Home Page**, and select from the list of great composers, or from the complete alphabetic list of composers

7 When you click on your chosen piece, a shortcut link to the file will be downloaded onto your hard disk

8 Double click the file to start the music in the appropriate player

6 Arts and Crafts

Whether you want to view pictures and drawings by contemporary artists or old masters, or get help and advice for creating your own works of art, the Internet has information and a host of tutorials to help you improve your skills.

Web Gallery of Art

The Web Gallery of Art is a virtual museum and searchable database of European painting and sculpture:

 Go to the website **www.wga.hu** and click the **Enter Here** button

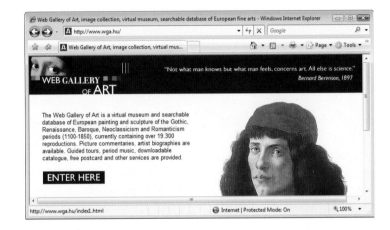

78

 Type the artist and title (e.g. Vermeer, Girl with a Pearl Earring) and the date or format if known, then press **Search** to find matching pictures

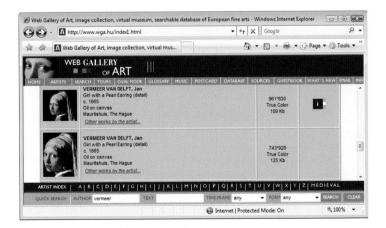

 Click the Info button for comments and reviews. Click the preview image to see the picture or detail full size

Visit the Sistine Chapel

To see the features of the Gallery in action, it is useful to take one of the predefined guided tours.

1 Click the title of the tour you wish to take, for example **Visit to the Sistine Chapel** in the Vatican

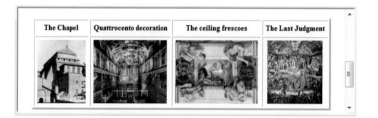

Guided Tour #5
Visit to the Sistine Chapel in Vatican
Start

2 Select a section of the tour to see detailed images and instructive comments

3 Some sections may be further subdivided, so you can explore in greater detail. You can even select a part of the ceiling of the Sistine Chapel to expand it and view it in greater detail

Continue the tour to study systematically the ceiling frescoes.

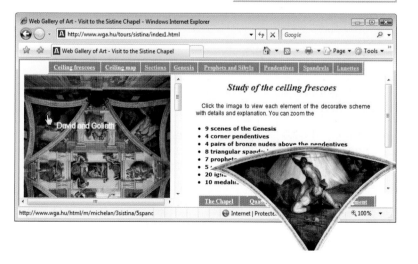

Hot tip

Click the Tours button to show brief details of the guided tours available.

TOURS

Don't forget

There are 15 different tours defined on the website, including:
#1 Italian painters
#2 European sculptors
#3 Art of Giotto
#4 Frescoes at Arezzo
#5 Sistine Chapel
#6 Brancacci Chapel

Hot tip

This tour shows how you click parts of the image to zoom in and see details and explanations. Other tours demonstrate more facilities such as dual mode (side by side) presentations.

Water Color Painting

If you are interested in learning to paint in water color, or want to develop your skill, there are websites to help you.

1 At **www.watercolorpainting.com** there are tutorials, step by step guides and lots of art related links

2 Click the **Tutorials** tab for an introduction to water color painting and for basic and advanced tutorials

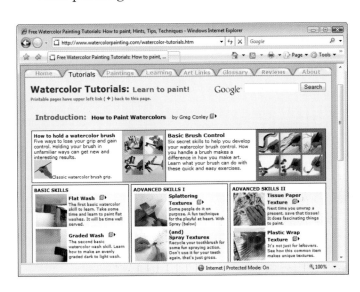

3 Click **Paintings** for step by step painting guides, explaining the materials and the techniques used

Learn to Draw

Perhaps you've always wanted to draw, but never had the time. Now may be just the time to begin.

1 Search for the phrase **learn to draw** for a list of websites related to this topic

2 Select **www.learn-to-draw.com**, to get sets of easy to follow instructions for a variety of drawing tasks

3 Pick the tutorial that suits your existing skill level or interest

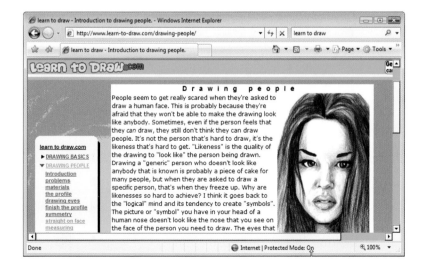

Don't forget

There are certain to be many websites offered. Some are purely for profit, some are there just to share an interest, while others turn out to be a mixture of both.

Beware

The Drawing Basics instructions are free, but the later topics in Drawing People and Draw Caricatures are available only to subscribers (who pay a one-time $16.95 charge).

DRAWING PEOPLE
Introduction
problems
materials
the profile
drawing eyes
finish the profile
symmetry
straight on face
measuring
the eyes
the nose
the mouth
the smile
hair
3 quarters

Pen and Ink Drawing

There's a "step-by-step" tutorial available on the Virtual Portmeirion website that tells you how to produce pen and ink drawings based on photographs.

 Visit **www.virtualportmeirion.com/howto/** to see the list of steps involved in creating the drawing

82

 You will need some suitable drawing tools:
- An extra fine black rolling ball pen
- A black felt tip pen
- A black broad tip magic marker
- A regular HB grade pencil
- A blue leaded pencil (blue doesn't photocopy)

Each step contains detailed advice, with lots of useful tips and illustrative sketches. For example, in step 4 you learn how to draw eyes with reflective areas, positioned so that the subject is looking in the right direction

1
2
3
4

Origami

What will you do with all that paper from your painting and drawing practise? Origami, the art of paper folding, sounds the natural thing to try next.

1 As usual, search for related sites by typing the keyword **origami** in the Search box

2 Go to **origami.iap-peacetree.org/basic_folds.php** to see the basic folds and learn origami terms

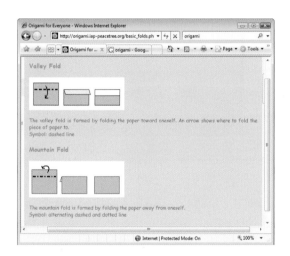

3 Alternatively, visit **www.origami.com/diagram.htm** for more than 300 models and clear diagrams in Adobe Acrobat format

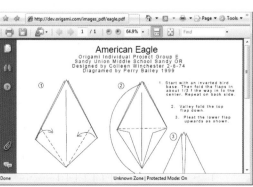

Hot tip

The Google search results may include images such as Origami diagrams, as well as relevant web pages – 17 million in this example.

Hot tip

The Origami Basics also explain base figures, the starting points for many models, and there are diagrams for some traditional models such as the Crane bird.

Celtic Knots

Celtic knots are motifs created by loops or continuous threads. They can be found on ancient stonework and in illuminated manuscripts, and in the form of jewellery and tattoos. You can also design and draw them on paper.

1 Go to **www.aon-celtic.com,** click the **Knotwork** link, then click the **Basic Celtic Knotwork** tutorial

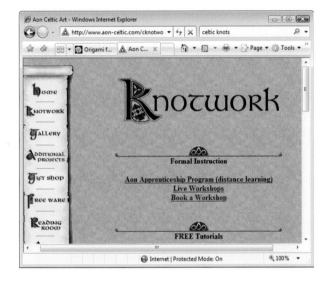

2 Follow the steps in the tutorial to mark up a piece of graph paper, joining the sections and the corners then deleting lines where threads overlap

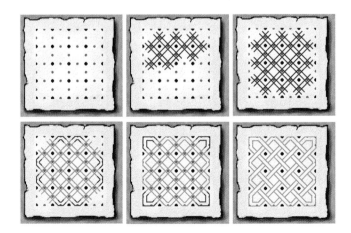

You can draw Celtic knots in your browser, with the help of applications provided on the Internet.

3 Go to **www.bit-101.com/celticknots** and click Draw to generate the Celtic knot as defined by the settings

4 Click on the cross-overs or adjacent segments to change the ways they are connected

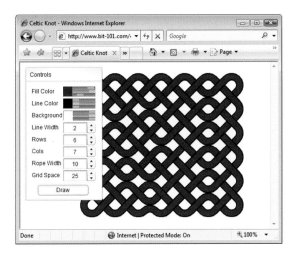

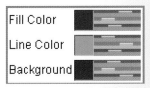
85

5 Visit **www.abbott.demon.co.uk/knots.html** for free, downloadable software to generate your own patterns

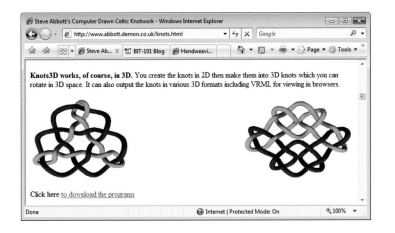

Cross Stitch

If your preference is for textiles and threads, you can find tutorials and patterns galore. These are often free of charge, even on websites that are online shops.

Hot tip

This website offers organic and fair trade alternatives for babies, adults and pets, but it does not sell cross stitch patterns and materials, so these are genuinely free.

Don't forget

The threads required are specified using DMC stranded cotton shade numbers.

Hot tip

Some sites offer .PDF versions of the patterns. These can be scaled on printing, allowing you to print a larger grid and make the symbols easier to read. Internet Explorer offers a similar option in its Print Preview menu.

1. Visit the site **www. birdcrossstitch.com** to display the free cross stitch patterns that are offered

2. Click on the image to display links for the pattern sheets

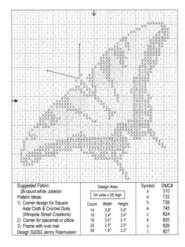

Suggested Fabric:		Design Area:		Symbol	DMC#
28-count white Jobelan		54 wide x 55 high		x	310
Pattern Ideas:				o	722
1) Corner design for Square		Count	Width	Height	h	726
Aida Cloth & Crochet Doily		14	3.9"	3.9"	e	745
(Wimpole Street Creations)		16	3.4"	3.4"	c	824
2) Corner for placemat or pillow		18	3.0"	3.1"	k	825
3) Frame with oval mat		22	2.5"	2.5"	v	826
Design ©2002 Jenny Rasmussen		28	1.9"	2.0"	t	827

3. The patterns specify the positions and suggest the most suitable colors for the stitches. Instructions also indicate the finished size using varying thread counts

Eastern Tiger Swallowtail Butterfly

When planning a butterfly garden, remember to use larval food plants. In Central Texas, an important larval food for the Eastern Tiger Swallowtail is the Mexican plum, which also provides nectar for butterflies and food for birds.

Bird Cross Stitch Designs by Jenny Rasmussen. Visit Jenny on the web at www.BirdCrossStitch.com

If you are new to cross stitch, a tutorial will help. Many cross stitch websites reference the very comprehensive tutorial written by Kathleen Dyer. To view a copy:

1 Go to **home.comcast.net/~kathydyer/index.html** and click the **Counted Cross Stitch Tutorial** link

2 The tutorial at **www.celticxstitch.ie/learnhow.html** offers a more graphical approach. They advise using a kit, but do tell you how to select your own materials

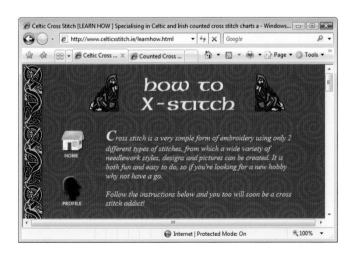

Don't forget

This tutorial covers all aspects of cross stitch, including:

Selecting the Fabric
Selecting the Thread
Selecting the Needle
Number of Strands
Making the X
Fractional Stitches
Cleaning and Storing
Mounting / Framing

87

Hot tip

The Celtic X-stitch tutorial has animated illustrations of the single, block and back stitches used for cross stitching.

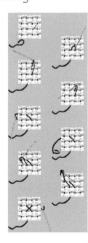

Knitting

If you enjoy knitting and like to make items for charitable causes, you'll find inspiration at websites such as Knitting Patterns Central at **www.knittingpatternscentral.com**.

Hot tip

The Free Pattern Directory lists about sixty categories, including afghans, bookmarks, coasters, hats, ponchos, teddy bears and toys, with numerous patterns in each.

Beware

Some patterns are in PDF format (*), and some patterns require registration before viewing (+).

- *Bookmark Leandra
- +Bookmark Pen Holder
- Diamond Lace Bookmark

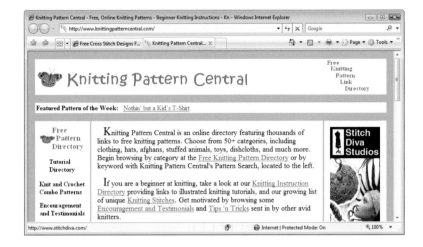

1 Select the pattern you want to review, for example the **Diamond Lace Bookmark**

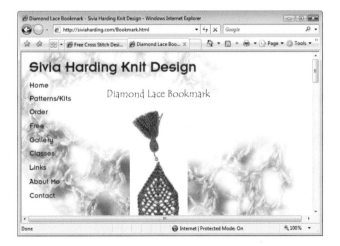

2 This gives details of the materials, full instructions for knitting and finishing, and permission to use the pattern for personal or charity purposes only

Hot tip

There are patterns available for all experience levels, and the website also provides a directory of instructions and tutorials for knitting techniques.

Guilds

Guilds are useful sources of information and let you contact like-minded people, over the Internet or in local meetings.

1 Visit the Knitting Guild Association (TKGA) at **www.tkga.com** and click on **Guilds/Clubs**

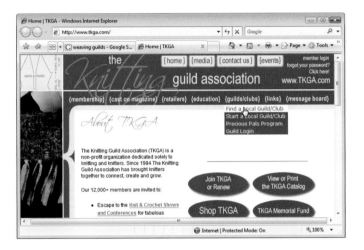

Don't forget

You'll find similar national associations for other countries and for most crafts and hobbies.

2 Select **Find a Local Guild/Club** and type your city or state (e.g. **Kansas**) to obtain a list for your area

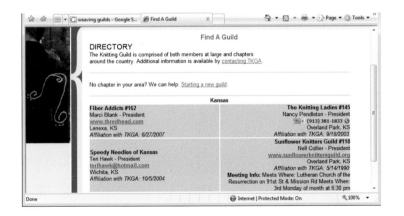

Hot tip

If there is no local guild or club in your area, the TKGA will advise and assist you in setting up your own local guild.

3 The guilds and clubs affiliated with TKGA in your area are listed, with contact names, telephone numbers and email address (where available)

Other Crafts

If we haven't covered your favorite craft, search on Google, or explore a website such as **www.about.com** that provides preselected links for particular subjects.

1. Click a category such as **Hobbies & Games**, and then a topic such as **Woodworking**, within the **Arts/Crafts** subcategory

2. Alternatively, the website **www.allfiberarts.com** covers textile handicrafts, including crochet, dyeing, felting, knitting, sewing, spinning and weaving

7 Travel Plans

The Internet provides you with the tools available to travel agents, so you can search for suitable deals, compare prices offered by different services, and create your own custom vacation. The Internet tells you what's going on at your chosen destination, and gives you maps to help you find your way there.

World Wide Travel

There's a whole wide world of travel options available to you when you start planning a trip. You could be seeking a low cost holiday or have a luxury vacation in mind. You might have plenty of time for research or it could be a last-minute trip. Safety and comfort could be your key consideration or you might be seeking adventure.

Don't forget

People over 50 make up the majority of travellers worldwide. They have the time and the freedom to travel, and with the help of the Internet, can find options to match their interests and their budgets.

Hot tip

Which are the best websites for travel? Each will have its own particular strengths, so it all depends on what aspects you consider important, how much of the work you are ready and able to do for yourself, and what time you have available for planning. We start by looking at the multifunction online travel agent sites (see page 93).

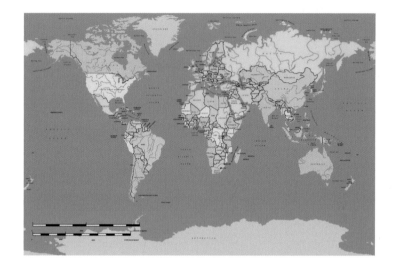

Whatever your requirements, the World Wide Web can help. There are many websites on the Internet devoted to one or more of the various aspects of travel, including:

- Transportation – air, sea, rail, road and river

- Accommodation – hotel, motel, b&b, self catering apartment, recreational vehicle, tent, camp site

- Destinations – domestic, overseas, remote location, single center, multicenter, tour, cruise

- Activities – sun and sand, sight seeing, city break, educational, cultural, sport, adventure, volunteer

- Information – maps, directions, guides, reviews, travel books, Internet access

- Facilities – itineraries, luggage, disabled suitability, currency, passports, adapters

Online Travel Agents

The most natural choice, when you first start planning vacations on the Internet, is to use the online equivalent of the high street travel agent. There are a number of such websites, but **Expedia** is a popular choice.

1 Go to **www.expedia.com** (or the version for your location) to research, plan and purchase your trip

2 Select Sign In and, on your initial visit click Create an Account. Fill in your name, user name, password and your email address

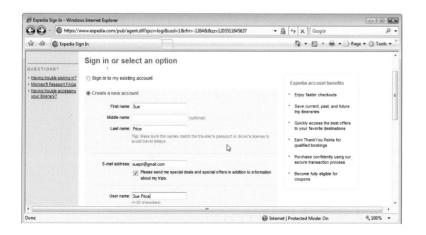

Beware

You can only purchase tickets and holidays from the version of the website meant for your home location i.e. www.expedia.

com	USA
co.uk	UK
ca	Canada
de	Germany
fr	France
it	Italy
nl	Netherlands
au	Australia

93

Hot tip

If you have signed up for a Microsoft Passport/Windows Live Id, you can use your Passport.

Hot tip

There are advantages to creating an account. You can enjoy faster checkouts, save itineraries and earn loyalty points and bonus coupons.

Book Flights

Most travel plans start with the flights, since these are often the limiting factor, due to their cost or the limited availability of seats on popular or holiday dates.

1 At **www.expedia.com**, select Flight, then Leaving From city or airport and Going to city or airport

2 Set the departure and return dates and times, and select the numbers of adults, seniors (65+) and children

3 Click **Search for Flights**

If there's more than one airport for the city, Expedia prompts you with a list, and searches for suitable flights.

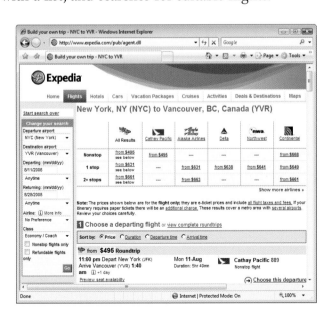

94

You select your departing flight from the first list, and then
select your returning flight from the next list. If you'd prefer
to select the two flights at once:

Choose a departing flight or view complete roundtrips

1. Click the link **view complete roundtrips,** to show all
the combinations of departing and returning flights

2. Check the details then click **Choose this flight** for
the roundtrip that you wish to book

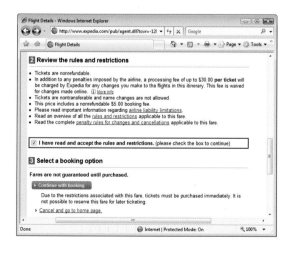

Book Your Hotel

You can choose to book a hotel while you are purchasing your flight tickets, or you can make it a separate transaction.

Don't forget

You may make additional savings if you purchase flights and book your hotel or rental car in the same transaction, but you'll have less flexibility.

Hot tip

You can specify a more exact destination, if you wish, to focus in on the area you are visiting.

1 At **www.expedia.com**, select Hotel, then the Destination city

2 Set the check-in and the check-out dates and times, and select the number of rooms and the number of adults and children

3 Optionally, specify a hotel name or class (1 to 5 star)

4 Click **Search for hotels** to list the hotels in the vicinity of the city, with room types and rates

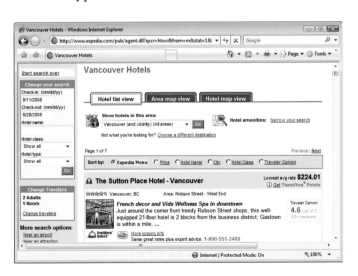

Don't forget

The rates may include exclusive, limited time offers for Expedia customers. These require full payment at the time of booking.

5 Click **Hotel map view** to select your hotel by location

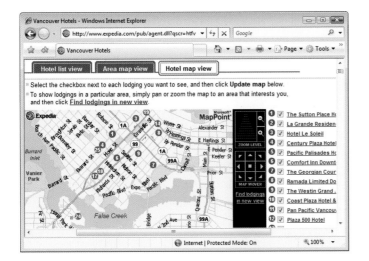

Hot tip

Zoom in and pan to the area that interests you, then click Find Lodgings In New View.

6 Select the hotel that best suits your needs, then click **Book it** to complete the order or save the booking in your itinerary

Book it

Other Hotels

Expedia only searches hotels where it has agreements. For example, it doesn't include hotels from the Intercontinental chain (Holiday Inn etc). For such hotels, you need to book direct with the chain or the specific hotel.

Beware

Check the restrictions carefully. You may be required to make full payment, and you may not be able to amend or cancel the booking.

97

Hot tip

If you book with any Intercontinental hotel, consider joining their Priority Club Rewards scheme. Other hotels have similar schemes (see page 100).

Book a Rental Car

You can book a rental car along with your flight tickets, or in a separate transaction.

1 At **www.expedia.com**, select Car, then the Pick-up location and Car type

2 Choose the pick-up and the drop-off dates and times, and set additional options such as one-way rentals if appropriate

3 Click **Search for cars**

Preferred Vendor View shows cars from companies with whom Expedia has special agreements. The other views show cars from all the available suppliers.

4 Click **Select** to see the full details for a particular car. Charges are shown in local currency, e.g. $Canadian

5 Continue the booking to confirm the driver details and book the car, or save the details in your itinerary

Hot tip

Choose from the list of vehicles in Car type, and Expedia will show cars that size or larger.

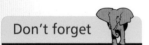

Hot tip

Expedia indicates the location of the rental car desk and if a shuttle bus is required.

Don't forget

You can also book directly with the car rental company. This may give you better pick-up and drop-off options.

Other Online Travel Agents

Like **Expedia**, **www.travelocity.com** website helps you book flights, hotels, cars, package vacations and cruises. It produces similar results, but not necessarily identical pricing.

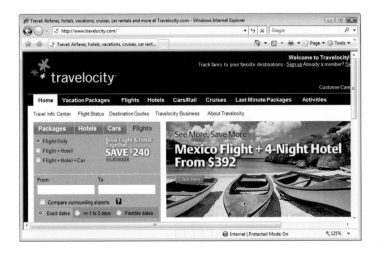

www.orbitz.com, a subsidiary of five American airlines, can book hotels, cars, packages and cruises, as well as flights.

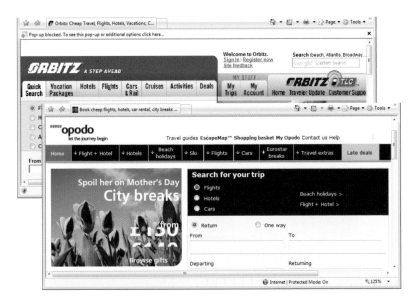

If you are based in Europe, you might consider **Opodo**, set up by nine European airlines, and providing a full range of travel planning services.

Hot tip

If you have the time, run the same travel query on several of the travel agent websites and explore the differences.

Hot tip

Orbitz is owned by American, Continental, Delta, Northwest and United airlines. This doesn't seem to limit its selections, and it does offer a low fare promise and a low price guarantee.

Hot tip

Opodo is now owned by the travel company Amadeus and the airlines Aer Lingus, Air France, Alitalia, Austrian Airlines, British Airways, Finnair, Iberia, KLM and Lufthansa.

Loyalty Cards

Beware

Keep track of the members of an alliance, since they will change. Aer Lingus is set to withdraw from the OneWorld alliance in 2007, while Japan Airlines, Malév and Royal Jordanian will be joining.

Don't forget

Some booking options from Expedia and other such sites may exclude loyalty card air miles and points, so you should take this into account when selecting between alternatives.

Hot tip

All loyalty programs include elite levels such as silver or gold, awarded when you attain a certain number of air miles or points during the membership year.

Airlines operate programs to encourage travelers to stay loyal to the particular airline or alliance of airlines. For example, American Airlines operates its own AAdvantage program, and participates in the OneWorld program with British Airways, Cathay Pacific, Qantas and other airlines.

Hotels also offer loyalty programs, which earn miles (in collaboration with airline programs) or points that can be exchanged for accommodation or other goods and services.

Car rental companies also offer loyalty programs, which can be linked to various hotel and airline programs.

Hertz #1 Club ■
Hertz #1 Club Gold ■

Last-Minute Bookings

Last-minute booking is perhaps the complete antithesis of loyalty programs – you have to take whatever you can get.

1 Visit website **www.priceline.com**, to show all the combinations of departing and returning flights

2 Enter the details then click **search now** to list the flights available from up to ten airlines

3 You'll also be offered the option to rent a car, plus a list of local attractions and services

Hot tip

If you can fly any time of day, agree to fly on any major airline, stay in any name-brand hotel or rent from any of the top five US car rental agencies, you might be able to save a lot of money.

Hot tip

There's a similar service to Priceline. com available from www.hotwire.com.

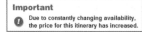

Beware

Prices may rise, even if you are in the middle of confirming the offer. However, you won't be obliged to complete the transaction.

Important
Due to constantly changing availability, the price for this itinerary has increased.

Name Your Own Price

With **Priceline.com** and **Hotwire.com**, you could make a bid for flights by specifying your own price and seeing if any airline is willing to accept it. Since you provide the price, not the supplier, this is known as a **reverse auction**.

Don't forget

Your flight could start any time between 6am and 10pm on your travel date, so you do need to be very flexible.

Not Flexible?
Choose exact flight times and prices

1 Request flights at **www.priceline.com**, entering the details and clicking **search now**, as described on page 101

2 Choose **Name Your Own Price**, then select departure and arrival airports you are willing to use

Hot tip

Your price is per round ticket, before taxes and fees. Click the link for Taxes and fees to discover just what taxes might be applied.

3 Provide the price that you are willing to pay for the journey that you have specified, and enter the passenger names

Beware

If the price is too low, your bid is rejected. If any airline is willing to accept your price, your bid will be accepted and your credit card will be charged. You won't know the details until you're fully committed.

4 When you are completely sure that the deal as defined would be acceptable to you, provide your credit card details and complete the bid

Travel Guide

To help you choose your destination and stop off points, you need a travel guide that will tell everything you need to know, laid out in a good and consistent format.

1 Go to **www.mytravelguide.com**, and type your destination e.g. **Vancouver, BC** in the Search box

Hot tip

MyTravelGuide lists related destinations, so you can select the most appropriate one.

2 The guide gives details such as hotels, attractions, restaurants and nearby towns for each location

Don't forget

MyTravelGuide is owned by Priceline, but it is completely free to use. If you register, you can create quick links and save your itineraries.

3 You will also find a detailed city map

Travel Directions

If you are planning a multi-stop driving vacation, you'll want travel directions as well as a map. Use a website that allows you to specify intermediate points on your journey.

1   Visit **www.randmcnally.com** and click **Road Explorers**

2   Click Join Now and sign up for the Basic Membership (which is free)

3   Provide your first and last name, email address, password, zip or post code, and date of birth

4   Once registered, click **Plan a Road Trip.** (You are now signed in as a member)

5   Supply a name for the route and indicate if children will be in the party. Click **Continue**

Plan a Road Trip

1 Enter the starting point address, or just city and state

2 Put the destination point details next

3 Optionally provide starting and ending dates for your trip

4 For a roundtrip, it creates the return route for you

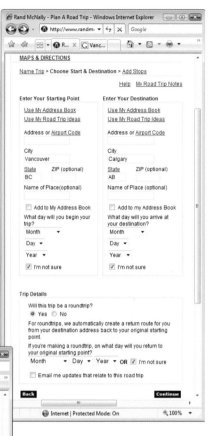

Hot tip

If the address is not completely defined, you may see a list of possible locations from which you can choose.

Don't forget

If the route suggested is not exactly what you want, you could introduce an extra stopover, e.g. you might add Lillooet between Whistler and Kamloops.

5 Click **Continue**, and the trip so far is displayed

6 Click **Add a Stop** and enter the address and optionally the arrival date for a stopover point

7 Click **Continue**, and add any further stopover points required

Print Trip Guide

When you have completed the route you can save it. Up to ten such routes can be saved at the website. You can view, edit or print the saved trips whenever you wish.

5-Day Forecast for Whistler, BC

Today
Mostly Sunny.
High 78. Low 54.

1 When you print the route, add "Step-by-Step directions"

2 You can also add weather data for each of the stop points

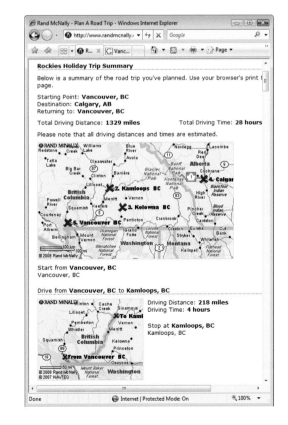

8 Explore Your Family Tree

The Internet has created a whole new way to search for information on your family background and your ancestors. You can share information with other parts of the same family, without having to travel around, even if your ancestral roots are from far distant shores.

Introduction to Genealogy

Don't forget

Other equivalent terms are ancestry, forebears, descent, lineage and pedigree, though that last term is usually associated with non-human groupings.

Beware

Genealogy research can turn into an obsession, as you reach further back in time, to solve puzzles and discover facts that others have missed.

Hot tip

You can download versions of these forms to print and complete manually, or to fill out using your computer software (see details on page 111).

The term Genealogy applies to the study of the history of past and present members of a particular family. It also applies to the records and documentation that describe that history, the members of the family and their relationships.

Genealogy is highly popular right across the world. There are many reasons why you might research your family's history:

- Simple curiosity about yourself and your roots
- Make your children aware of their ancestors
- Preserve family cultural and ethnic traditions
- Medical family history (inherited disease or attribute)
- Join a lineage or heritage society

Getting started is generally quite easy – you find the oldest living members of your family and ask them about other members, especially those who are no longer here to answer for themselves.

After the first flush of success however, it could become difficult to fill in the gaps and extend the history further back in time. You have to rely on official records, and this could require a lot of travel, especially if your family originated overseas. Fortunately, much of the necessary legwork can now be accomplished over the Internet, there's plenty of advice and guidance, and you'll be able to capitalize on the research that others have carried out.

The information you glean can be recorded on charts designed to organize genealogical data.

- Ascendant, Ahnentafel and Pedigree charts
- Descendant, Progenitor charts
- Family Group sheets

These forms and the way to use them are described in various tutorials (see page 109).

Researching Your Family Tree

If you are new to genealogy, perhaps the best place to start is with an online (and free) genealogy tutorial.

1 There's a tutorial "Researching Your Family Tree" at **www.learnwebskills.com/family/intro.html** which provides a self-paced introduction

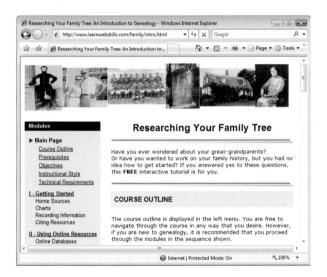

Follow the modules in this tutorial to research your own ancestors while learning to use the genealogical charts, online databases and other resources

2 You can communicate with other users of the tutorial through the Yahoo group **Learngen**. The tutorial includes instructions for joining this group

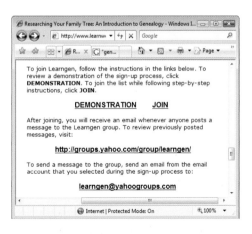

Hot tip

Search Google for "Genealogy Tutorial" (the quotes mean the exact phrase), and you get 1850 matching web pages.

Hot tip

The navigation bar on the left lists the contents of the six modules, plus more than 20 useful website links.

Don't forget

The Tools section has links to charts and tools (see page 111).

Genealogy 101

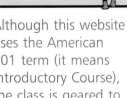

Don't forget

Although this website uses the American 101 term (it means Introductory Course), the class is geared to genealogy researchers in all countries, not just the US.

Hot tip

Scroll down to subscribe to the "About Genealogy Tip of the Day" email newsletter for updates as other classes become available.

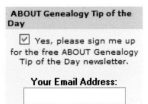

1 For a somewhat more structured introduction, go to **genealogy.about.com** and click **Genealogy 101**

2 Scroll down to the **Learning Corner** and click the **Intro to Genealogy Class** link:

This class currently consists of four lessons:

- Genealogical Basics
- Family & Home Sources
- Genealogy Research 101
- Vital Records – Birth, Marriage, Divorce, Death

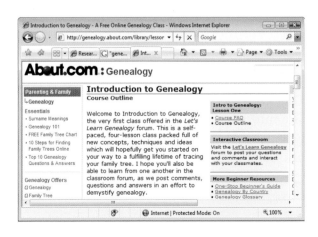

Genealogy Charts

1 Go to **www.ancestry.com** (a site suggested by both tutorials) and click the **Learning Center** button

Don't forget

Most genealogy websites will have free charts available. There are also many commercial products on offer.

2 In the Topics section, on the right, select **Print a Family Tree Chart**

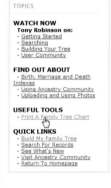

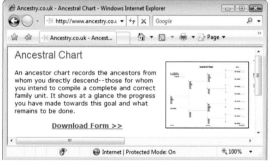

Don't forget

You may need to install the Adobe Reader to view and print the charts (see page 74).

3 Click **Download Form** to view or print the PDF form in your browser, or right-click and select **Save Target As...** to save the file on your hard disk

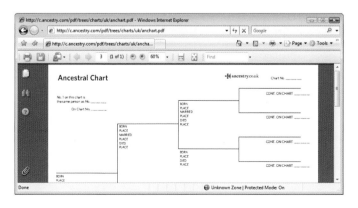

Hot tip

The Ancestry.com family tree resources also include a family group form, census forms for the US, UK and Canada, and other record forms.

Charts in Text Format

If you want to complete your genealogy forms on your computer, you need the forms in a text format.

1 At the Family Tree website **www.familytreemagazine.com**, click the **free research forms** link found in the Tool Kit

Download Forms
Free research forms, ancestor charts, census forms and more!

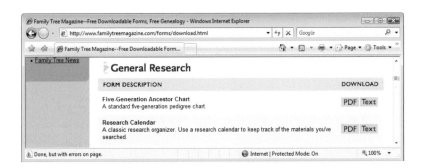

2 This displays the Forms Download area, where you will find PDF and Word versions of the charts

3 Click **Text** and follow the prompts to download the file to your hard disk

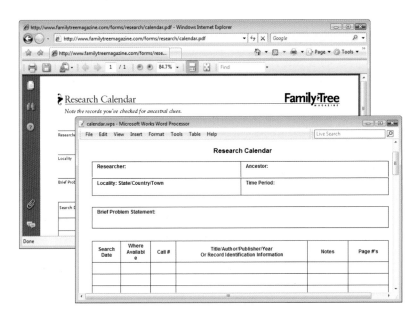

Vital Records

When you've collected all the information you can from family members, and organized it using genealogy charts, you'll have a list of unanswered questions, and you'll need to start searching records to find some of the answers.

There are two main types of genealogical records that you can investigate:

Original records

An original record is an account of a specific event, written at or near the time the event took place. Historically, many civil and religious authorities kept records on events in the lives of people in their jurisdictions. Original records include:

- Vital Records (birth, marriage, divorce and death)
- Church Records (christenings, baptisms, confirmations, marriages, or burials)
- Cemetery Records (names, dates and relationships)
- Census Records (household member name, sex, age, country or state of birth, occupation)
- Military, Probate, Immigration Records

Compiled records

A compiled record is a collection of information on a specific person, family group or topic. Compiled records exist because others have already researched original records or collated information from other compiled records or other sources. Compiled records include:

- Ancestral File (over 13 million names, linked into ancestors and descendants)
- International Genealogical Index (computerized index of over 187 million names extracted from birth, christening, marriage, and other records)
- Published Family Histories, Biographies, Genealogies, and Local Histories

Hot tip

You may be able to access original records on microfiche, and some, especially census records, have been indexed and computerized. See page 116.

Don't forget

Compiled records are useful if you want to learn about ancestors who were born before 1900, but are not likely to have information about modern families.

Hot tip

The two main compiled record files were developed by the family history department of the Church of Latter-Day Saints (see page 115).

Cyndi's List

To find out where to look for original records, you should start at **www.cyndislist.com**, a search engine that is dedicated to genealogical research via the internet. You can search for helpful websites by location or by record type.

 Click **Beginners** in the main category index, and you'll be able to view lists of websites related to researching various types of original and vital records

2 **Researching: Census Records** gives lists of USA and worldwide census sites, plus details on Soundex indexing

FamilySearch

The **www.familysearch.org** website owned and operated by the Church of Latter-day Saints provides free family history.

Don't forget

Advanced Search lets you add parent and spouse names for a particular ancestor.

1. The minimum information you need provide is the surname. The exact spelling isn't essential

2. Select a record type (life event) for which you have the year (exact, or give or take 2, 5, 10 or 20 years)

3. Choose the country, and (for Canada and the US) the state

4. Matching records are displayed. Review the records, to confirm you have identified the correct person

Hot tip

The records found will provide you with further clues about the person and family, perhaps including, as in this case, a pedigree chart, with links back to further charts.

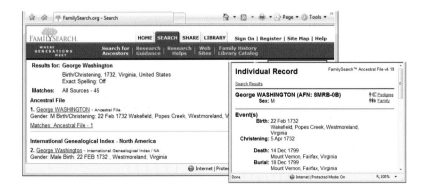

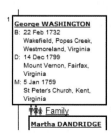

Ancestry.com

Don't forget

If you are interested in Canadian data, evaluate Ancestry.ca instead. For United Kingdom data, try Ancestry.co.uk. You can sign on at either website using your Ancestry.com guest account.

You can search for ancestors at **www.ancestry.com**. This website has many databases, including census, birth, marriage, death, military and immigration. It offers paid membership subscriptions, but there is a free Registered Guest account, which allows you to receive the free newsletter and build an online family tree, and access some of the databases.

1 At **www.ancestry.com**, select Help and type **Guest** in the Search box then click the Search button

Beware

The Guest membership is well hidden, so you need to issue a search to find the details.

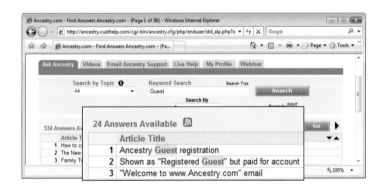

2 Select the article **Ancestry Registered Guest Account** for details, and select Click Here to sign up

Don't forget

Make a note of your user name and password for future access. On this occasion you are immediately signed in.

Overview of Guest registration

To use any of the features on Ancestry, a user must have at least a Guest registration. To create a registered guest account, click here. As a Registered Guest, a limited number of resources are available at no cost. These can be created by providing a first and last name and an email address. Registered Guest accounts have been put in place to allow members to:

3 Register your details and your guest user name and password will be displayed

4 Search for one of your ancestors, giving all the details that you have available

Don't forget

Most of the databases that appear on the Historical Records page are locked and only available to subscribers.

🔒 17 Virginia Census, 1607-1890
🔒 16 1870 United States Federal Census

5 You'll see a list of databases with matching entries

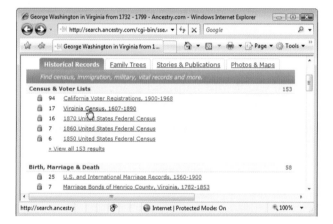

6 You can view details in the free databases, but when you try to obtain details from a members-only database, you'll be invited to sign up for the 14 day free trial

Beware

The guest account allows you to explore the databases, without having to use up the time on your 14 day free trial until you are ready to proceed in earnest. However, to enable your free trial, you must provide credit card details and sign up for a minimum period.

7 You'll be asked for your details and a credit card. If you wish to subscribe, choose between US or Worldwide membership

117

US National Archives

Some of the answers to your questions may be found in the US National Archives at the website **www.archives.gov**.

1 Select the **Genealogists/Family Historians** link where you'll find help and guidance to get started

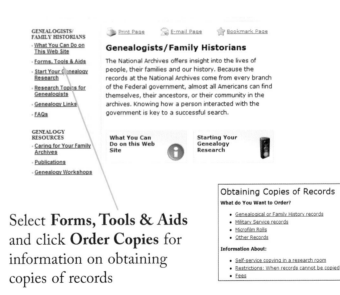

2 Select **Forms, Tools & Aids** and click **Order Copies** for information on obtaining copies of records

3 You may have to visit in person for some of your research (or hire an independent researcher to work on your behalf)

Other National Archives

Other countries will of course have their own equivalent to the US National Archives. For Australian information, go to **www.naa.gov.au**, and click **Services, For family historians.**

You'd visit **www.collectionscanada.ca/** for Canadian records.

The UK has its records at **www.nationalarchives.gov.uk**.

Don't forget

Any person is entitled to visit the archives and use its services. You don't need to be an Australian citizen or resident.

Hot tip

There's a link to the Canadian Genealogy Center, which offers genealogical content, services, advice and research tools.

Hot tip

The UK site has an explicit Family History section with expert advice on using the archives to build up your family tree.

Immigrant Records

If your family origins are from overseas, you will need to find the connection between the two family groups. Immigration records may be the answer.

The website **www.immigrantships.net** makes passenger lists available for a number of ships, though it is important to remember that it was 1820 before the federal government began requiring passenger lists from ship captains.

Don't forget

You'll find immigrant records for earlier dates in the US immigration databases at Genealogy.com

John Washington found in:
Passenger and Immigration Index, 1500s-1900s
 More Information

Hot tip

Castle Garden was the landing port before Ellis Island, for 1851-1891. Records for this period are found in Genealogy.com.

Ellis Island, just off Manhattan Island, New York, became the gateway to the United States from 1892 to 1924, during which time over 20 million immigrants passed through the immigration station. The website is **www.ellisisland.org**.

9 Digital Photography

Find advice and guidance on the Internet to improve your skill and technique. Store and backup your digital photographs and print online photos. Share your photos with your friends and family, and view the results obtained using various cameras and lenses.

Tips on the Internet

If you use a digital camera, the Internet becomes a natural extension. It offers a wide range of digital photographic information, facilities and tools. These may be provided by institutions such as colleges and libraries, equipment manufacturers, individuals, enthusiasts or professional photographers.

To start with, there are websites that tell you how to improve your digital photography skills and techniques.

1. Fuji has some tips for better photographs and a useful glossary, at **www.fujifilm.com/support**

2. There's a rather more comprehensive website offered by Kodak. Go to **www.kodak.com** and click **Consumer Products** and then **Tips & Projects Center**

3. Review all the entries in **Tips, Projects & Ideas, Educational Topics** and **Inspirational Stories** and visit some of the web pages from the list of most popular pages

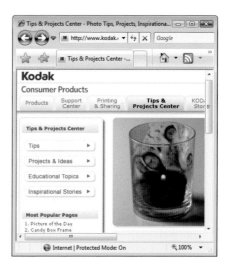

Tutorials

There are numerous tutorials on various aspects of digital photography, some for beginners, for example those at the ShortCourses website:

1 Switch to **www.shortcourses.com/workflow** for a short course on digital photography workflow

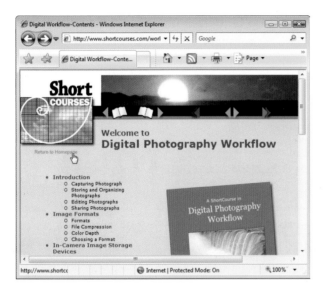

Hot tip

Click the Homepage link to see the full list of the short courses that are on offer. You can view them freely online, or download a PDF version (for a fee).

2 If you are ready for a challenge, view the tutorial **Making fine prints in your digital darkroom,** at the **www.normankoren.com** website

Don't forget

Click the Tutorials on Photography link (or add the #Tutorials bookmark to the website address) to display the list of tutorials.

Hot tip

This is a multi-part series that introduces tools and techniques for making fine prints digitally, to meet the highest aesthetic and technical standards.

Find Inspiration

Digital photography is not just about equipment and techniques, it is also about subject and composition. Perhaps the best way to explore these aspects is through viewing the work of other photographers, for example at the Photographic Society of America.

1 Visit **www.psa-photo.org** to see a series of examples. Click the **Galleries** link to select a gallery and choose members by name to view their work

2 The Royal Photographic Society allows members to upload their portfolios to the Society website. They can be viewed at **www.rps.org/portfolios.php**

Share Photos Online

You can use the Internet to share your digital photographs. You don't have to join a society and create a portfolio, and the photographs can be private, just for friends and family.

1 Visit **www.ofoto.com** and click the **Get Started** link

Hot tip

Kodak runs Ofoto so the address becomes www.kodakgallery.com and you can use either address to visit the website.

2 Enter first name, email ID, password, cell phone (optional). No credit card is needed. Click **Create Account**

3 Your gallery is assigned, and a confirming email is sent to the email ID you provided

4 You are now ready to upload photographs

Don't forget

If you are located outside the US, click the Change link and select your country before registering, to get local prices and shipping charges.

125

Upload Photographs

Hot tip

You might find it more useful to put the date you took the photos, rather than the date you created the album.

Don't forget

If your images are saved in a format other than .jpg, you must use an image editing application to convert the files, before you upload.

Beware

Low resolution may be fine for the web, but they may be unsuitable for printing, so you may get a warning message.

---

1. Click the **Upload Photos** button to create a new album

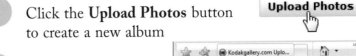

2. Provide album name, create date and brief description, then click **Continue**

3. Follow the prompts to install the **Easy Upload** software (see page 174)

(see page 174)

4. Click **Add Pictures** and choose images (.jpg only) from your photo folder

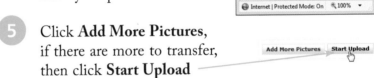

5. Click **Add More Pictures**, if there are more to transfer, then click **Start Upload**

6. Thumbnails are dropped from the holding area as each image is transferred. There's also a progress bar

7. When the upload completes, carry on with the next action e.g. upload another album

View Albums

1 Sign in to Kodak Gallery (or click **My Gallery** if you are already signed in) to list your albums

2 Click an album to display thumbnails of its contents

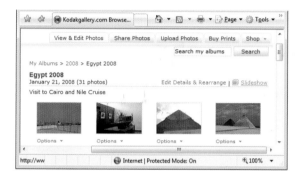

3 Click **Edit Details & Rearrange** to make changes, or click **Slideshow** to view the photos in turn

4 Click any thumbnail to jump to that position

Hot tip

Click the Options link below a thumbnail and select View Larger, to edit the photo title, or make changes to the image.

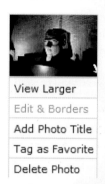

Don't forget

Select Options, Edit & Borders, to adjust the images before printing them (see page 130).

Share Albums

You can invite your friends and family to view your digital photographs, by sending them an email.

1   Click the **Share Photos** tab and choose an album, then click the Select Album button

2   The album is added to the list of albums that are available for sharing

3   When you've added all the albums you want to share, click **Next**

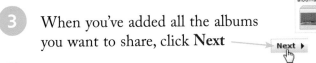

4   Enter the email address and amend the message if desired, then click the **Send Invitation** button

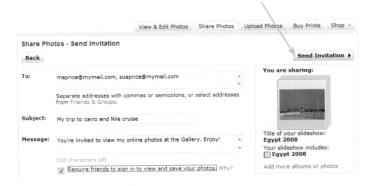

5   Your friends click the **View photos** link in their email, and then sign in

You're invited to view my online photos at the Gallery. Enjoy!
- Ineasysteps

View photos

View Friends' Albums

If your friends upload digital photographs, they can invite you to share their albums, by sending you an email.

129

Hot tip

When you receive invitations to view slideshows, you will have the ability to share their photos with other friends and family.

① Click the **View Photos** link in your email, and sign in to view their slideshows

② When you click **Exit Slideshow**, their albums are added to your gallery, in a separate Friends area

Don't forget

You can treat the shared photos just like your own and purchase prints, create a picture mug or order a framed picture etc. (see page 130).

③ Hover the mouse pointer over a shared album, to see your friend's name and the album title

Frame a photo · Create mugs

Order Prints

Kodak provides a printing service, which is their motivation for providing storage on the Internet. They keep the original image file (even though slideshows use reduced images) so prints will be full quality.

Hot tip

You can add all the photos from the album with a single click. You can then click to remove individual photos.

 Sign in and click **My Gallery**, open an album and click **Buy Prints**, then select the photos to print

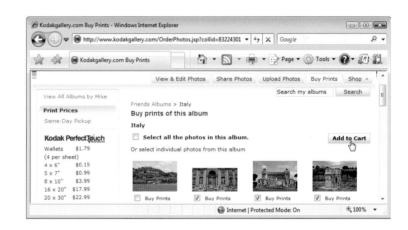

Hot tip

As well as normal prints, you can order posters, collages, frames, greetings cards, stickers, cards and calendars, plus mugs, bags, aprons and other items decorated with your photos.

2 When you've finished choosing, click **Add to Cart**

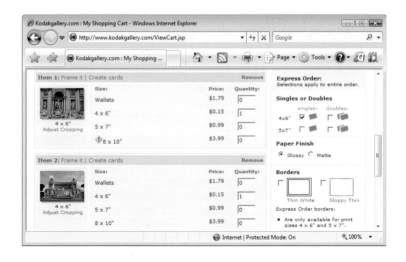

3 You can specify photo options individually, or choose the Express options for all the photos in your order

...cont'd

4 Click **Checkout** to specify shipping and payment

5 Provide the delivery address details (this could be your own or a friend's address)

6 Make this the default address, if appropriate, then click **Save**

7 The rates depend on the order size and the shipping speed that you request

8 Click **Next** to check the order summary. Click **Next** again and then add your credit card details, before you click **Place Order** to complete your purchase

Hot tip

You can arrange to pick up your order at a retail store. You'll pay a $1.49 fee, but no shipping charge. This applies to US website accounts only.

Beware

You will be charged prices and shipping based on the website where you register (see page 125). If you are UK based, but have a US account, you'll pay international shipping.

Storage and Backup

The EasyShare Gallery provides free, unlimited online photo storage for 12 months from the date of your first upload, and will store the photos online for as long as your account is active. That means making at least one purchase from the Gallery every 12 months.

You can preserve your entire photo collection on disc with Archive CDs. These contain a separate file for each photo, at the resolution in which it was uploaded.

132

1 Click the **Shop** tab, then click the **Archive CDs** entry in the **Products** list

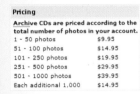

2 Gallery Premier provides a personal homepage, and also maintains your photo storage (without further purchases) while the subscription is in effect

Yahoo Photos

There are other websites that offer free, online photo storage, Flickr for example. This requires you to have a Yahoo ID to sign up (see page 137 to create a free Yahoo ID).

1 Go to **www.flikr.com** and click **Create Your Account**

2 Sign in to Yahoo using your existing ID and password

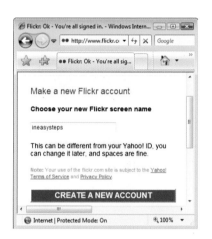

3 Choose your Flikr screen name then click **Create a new Account**

4 Click **Upload your first photo** to get started, or click the **Explore Flickr** link

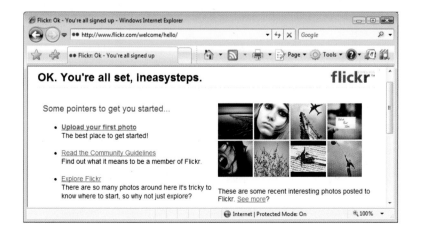

Hot tip

With a free Flickr account, you can upload 100MB of photos per month. However, only the latest 200 photos can be viewed. Flickr is most useful for sharing pictures of events such as a wedding or a celebration.

Don't forget

On Flikr, you can choose to make your photos private or public or make them available to groups of people with shared interests.

PBase Galleries

The PBase photo sharing and hosting site encourages public viewing, giving serious photographers the opportunity to display their skills to the world. You'll usually find information on the settings and equipment used, and lots of comments made by other viewers.

1 The PBase website is at **www.pbase.com**. Click **Popular Galleries** to view slideshows, or click the **Search** button to look for particular subjects

2 For example, a search for **Auroras** produced several pages of fascinating Northern Lights slideshows

10 Keep in Touch

Whether you are at home, or on vacation, the Internet helps you to keep in touch with your family and friends. You can send and receive email, exchange instant messages or send electronic greetings.

Email Communication

The Internet allows you to communicate with friends, family and business contacts quickly and easily, whether they are just down the street or on the other side of the world. You can send to individuals, or whole groups of people such as club members, with a simple click of the mouse button. You can include photographs with your email and attach all kinds of documents such as Minutes, Agendas and Reports.

Email requires two things – software that allows you to create, save, send and receive messages and an Internet connection.

The Software

Microsoft's Outlook and Windows Mail can both be used for email. They are programs that come with Office and Windows respectively. Outlook is a full Personal Information Manager which includes an email program. Windows Mail is a subset of Oulook which is just the email element.

However, many Internet Service Providers offer their own email facility. They allow you to create, send, receive, read and store your email on their server, using your browser. This is known as Webmail or sometimes Netmail. Its big advantage is that you can access your mail from anywhere in the world – from a friend's PC, a hotel or Internet cafe. It does, however, mean that you must be online when using it.

Web-based email

Each individual ISP offers their own mailbox structure, but they are all very similar in approach. If you are accustomed to using Outlook Express or Windows Mail, you will find the transition to a web-based facility very straightforward.

Some email accounts are normally web-based only, for example Hotmail and Yahoo. For the purposes of this book, we will be using Yahoo mail.

Don't forget

If you have a dial-up connection, you may prefer to use Outlook or Windows Mail at home as they allow you to compose and read your messages off-line, without paying for connection time. Email using Windows Mail is covered in depth in *Computing for Seniors in Easy Steps*.

Hot tip

When setting up your email account, check to see if your ISP allows Webmail, especially if you anticipate travelling and want to be able to keep in touch.

Create a Webmail Account

Your ISP may already provide you with a webmail account. However, if you need a new account, you can create one at Yahoo.com:

1 Start Internet Explorer, go to **www.yahoo.com** and click on the **Sign Up** next to Free mail

2 Enter your details. As you type, Yahoo explains how it uses the information

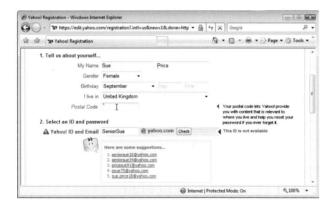

3 Type in your preferred choice of ID and click **Check**. If the ID is not available, Yahoo will suggest alternatives

4 Complete the registration details, then check and agree to the terms and conditions. Click **Create My Account**

Don't forget

Be sure to make a note of your ID and password and keep it in a safe place.

Hot tip

With so many people now using email, you may find that your preferred name has already been taken.

Don't forget

The verification process is used to prevent automated registrations. You must be able to read the monitor to type in the letters – something that can only be achieved with the human eye.

The Webmail Window

With your mail account now set up, connect to Yahoo.com and sign in.

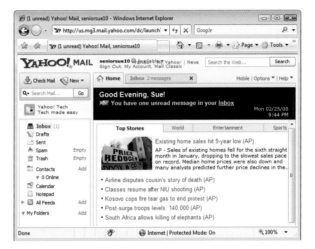

The Yahoo mail screen opens on the Home tab which provides current news items. The second tab, the Inbox tab, shows the number of new messages.

The Folders panel, on the left of the page, displays your current folders and allows you to organize your mail.

- the Inbox is where your mail arrives. To view your new mail, click on the Inbox folder, or the Inbox tab

- Drafts is where you will store any incomplete messages, or ones that you do not want to send immediately

- the Sent folder keeps a copy of email sent

- the Spam folder will contain any messages that the Yahoo spamguard program isolates as unwanted

- Trash contains any messages that are no longer required

- Contacts gives you access to your Contact list

- Calendar is a diary function

- Notes is a small memo function

Access Your Mail

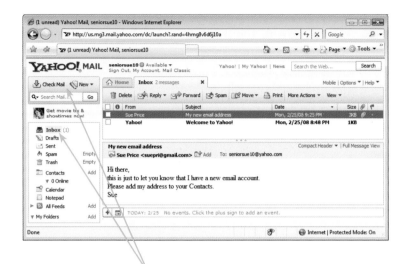

1 Click on **Check Mail** or the Inbox folder in the left panel to show new messages. The number (1) indicates that there is one new message

2 Click on the message subject to open the message. The message opens on a new tab

3 With the message open, select from the options to Delete, Reply, Forward, mark as Spam or move to another folder. Alternatively, you can select **Next** or **Previous** (message)

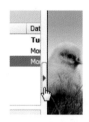
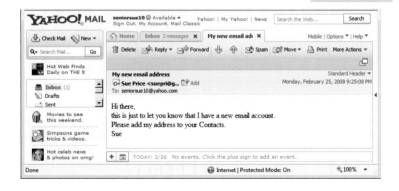

4 Click the **X** on the tab to return to the Inbox view

Create and Send Mail

1 Click **New** on the Mail window to create a new message, or click the down arrow and select Chat or Text message. The New Email Message window opens on a new tab

2 Select the recipient, either by typing their address, or by clicking on the **To:** button to add addresses from your Contacts

3 Press the Tab key or click in the Subject box and type in the topic of the email

140

4 Tab again to the message area which offers standard word processing tools, such as different font styles and spell checking. Type your message and click **Send**. You will get confirmation that the email has been sent

5 Click **OK**. The message tab will close and you will return to the Home tab

Manage Your Mail

Webmail ISPs allocate you storage space on their server when you sign up for their email facility. Yahoo for example, now gives you unlimited storage as long as you abide by normal email rules and do not abuse the system.

Sort your messages

1 Click in the header area on **Sender** or **Subject** to sort alphabetically, click again to sort in reverse order

2 Click **Date** to sort your messages newest to oldest or again to sort in reverse order

Hot tip

Sort your messages newest to oldest to have your new email appear at the top of the Inbox.

141

Manage your messages

1 Click in the box to the left of the message to select it (insert a tick). Click again to remove the tick. You can tick as many messages at a time as you wish. The messages can then be managed as one

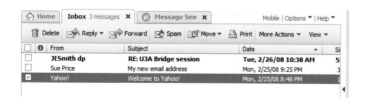

Hot tip

Tick the box next to Sender to select or deselect all messages.

Delete your messages

1 Click **Delete** to transfer all selected messages to the Trash folder. Messages in the Trash folder do not count towards your total storage

Don't forget

Messages will remain in the Trash folder, allowing you to reinstate them if necessary. Click on Empty to empty the Trash folder.

Create and Use Folders

To create folders for webmail storage:

1 Click **Add** next to My Folders in the side panel and the new folder will appear in the folder list

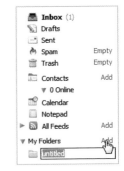

2 Type the folder name and click away from the folder name to create it. The new folder opens on a new tab

3 Click back on the Inbox in the folder list to open it

4 The next time you click the **Move** button, you will have the option to move selected items to the new folder

5 You can also drag and drop a message into a folder

6 To rename or delete a folder, right click on the folder and choose one of the options

7 You can Hide or Show your list of My Folders by clicking on the arrow symbol

Webmail Options

Customize your webmail account and take advantage of features offered by your ISP, using Options on the main Mail window and select **Mail**.

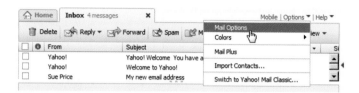

Spam

SpamGuard is on when you sign up to Yahoo. Click on Spam to change settings, such as how long to keep spam messages and where to move allowed messages.

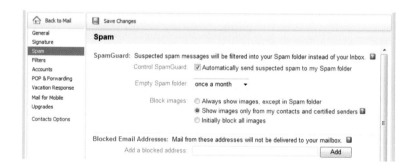

Blocked Addresses

This allows you to block messages from your Inbox for up to 500 addresses or domain names. The blocked messages will be deleted before you see them.

Filters

Filters are applied to your incoming mail. Use filters to automatically sort your mail into appropriate folders. Click on Filters, then Add and complete the details.

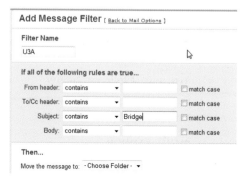

Hot tip

Other webmail options include adding an automatic signature, setting an auto response when you are away or on vacation and setting your general preferences.

Don't forget

Webmail providers will also offer more sophisticated functions, improved filters, larger amounts of storage etc. on a chargeable basis.

Attachments

You can attach documents and photos to your email with a webmail account.

1. Create your email in the usual way and click the button to **Attach Files**

2. The Documents folder will open. Select the file or navigate your PC's folders to locate and select the required file. Click Open. Repeat to attach more files

3. The file(s) will be checked for viruses. Complete your email and then send

4. Click **Remove** if you change your mind

Receive Attachments

When you receive a file with an attachment:

1 Check that you know the sender. If you are unsure of the source, then be on your guard

2 Open the message, the attachment will be indicated in the email header area

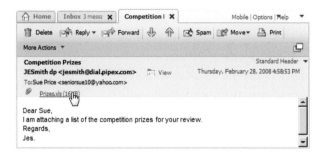

Beware

You should always scan attachments for viruses, even if you do know the sender. Yahoo webmail provides a virus scanner. Check your provider to see what it offers.

3 Click on the file name. The attachment will immediately be scanned for viruses and a status report given

145

Don't forget

You may need to select a new destination folder as the computer will remember the previous destination of a downloaded file and will open that folder automatically.

4 Click **Download Attachment**. You will have a further opportunity to Open or Save the attachment. Normally you would select **Save** and then choose the appropriate folder

E-Cards

You can send all kinds of free greeting cards to friends and family using the Internet. Do a search for free e-cards with your chosen search engine or visit the home page of a household name for greetings cards.

 Log on to **www.hallmarkcards. com** and click the link for Free E-Cards

 Choose a category and select a card from the illustrations. Free cards and animated cards will be labeled

E-postcards

Many tourist destinations have comprehensive websites, to advertise facilities, activities, hotels etc. Check these sites for digital postcards – a good way to stay in touch when travelling.

Instant Messaging

Many ISPs and other software companies provide Instant Messaging services. This service allows you to communicate with a selected list of contacts, either by typing your message, or by voice. With a camera attached to your PC, some instant messaging programs will even allow you to transmit (and receive) video.

For this you will need to download and install special software. In this example we shall use Skype, which is available at no charge and provides full video service.

Don't forget

You will need a full DSL (broadband) service to use Instant Messaging.

1. Visit **www.skype.com** and click the Download tab and then the **Download now** button

2. Save the file to a Downloads folder or to the Desktop. When the download is complete, open the folder and double-click the file to start the installation

3. Follow the on-screen instructions to choose the program location and other options. It is usually best to accept the defaults

Beware

Skype's on-screen instructions suggest that when you have downloaded the file you select to Run it. Their help page suggests you save it to the Desktop and Run later, a better option.

Sign Up to Skype

When you start Skype for the first time you will need to sign in and create an identity for yourself.

1 Open Skype and click **Don't have a Skype Name**. Supply a User name and password. As with the Yahoo ID, you may need to try several names to find one available

2 Then follow the on-screen instructions supplying an email address and your country

3 When you click Sign In the Getting Started tutorial opens. It steps through making a test call, adding Contacts and accessing other Skype offerings such as free calls and buying add-ons such as headphones

Add Contacts

To be able to use Skype you will need to create a list of Contacts. When you sign in for the first time, Skype offers to look through your Address Book to identify and copy those addresses it recognizes as having access to Skype.

When you wish to add other names from your Contacts list or a new Contact:

Hot tip

If your new contact does not have Skype, click Tools, Share Skype with a friend. Complete the form with your own and the friend's details. Your friend will receive an email to join, with an option to download the Skype Program.

1 In the main Skype window click **Add Contact**

2 Enter a new contact's details and click Find

3 Click to Add Skype Contact and complete the message to request their contact details

Don't forget

Whichever way you add your contacts, you will need to get a confirming response from them that they are happy to join your instant messaging community. The agreement of course works both ways – you will be asked if you wish to join their contact list.

Make a Call

Don't forget

If your contact has supplied a landline or mobile phone number and you click on that, Skype will presume that you wish to call that number, rather than connect via the Internet. You will need to purchase credit from Skype to use those methods.

Hot tip

Your contacts will be able to see if you are online. To change your status, click the small tick on the Status bar and select a different option, especially if you don't wish to be interrupted.

1. Your first call should be to check your installation, so double-click on **Skype Test Call**. You will hear a voice asking you to record a ten second message which will be played back to you if your system is working correctly

2. To connect with a friend, double-click their name or select their name and click on the green phone

3. You will hear a ringing tone. If they are online they will be informed that you are calling. If they are off-line, you will be informed

4. You can type your messages or with a microphone attached to your PC you will be able to have live conversations

5. With a video camera attached, click the **Start My Video** button to show your own image together with a larger video of your contact

6. Click to take the image full screen if required

7. Click the **History** tab to see a record of all calls to and from your PC, including those missed

11 Publish to the Internet

Become completely involved in the Internet phenomena by creating your own website, and let other web users visit your web pages. If you've got something to say, but don't want a complete website perhaps you could try your hand at blogging (writing a web log), or access feeds to stay up to the minute with website changes.

Don't forget

This topic is covered in-depth in another title from this series called *Building a Website for Seniors in Easy Steps*.

Hot tip

You do not need to be an Internet programmer to build a web page, and it needn't cost anything at all. However, if you aren't charged a fee, you may find adverts or links added to your web page.

Build a Web Page

If you have something to share, why not create your own page on the web? Think of things you might want to publish in your web page. It doesn't have to be for business. It could be just for fun, so you can learn first hand about the way the Internet operates. It might be a place where you store information related to a hobby or interest, that you'd like to share with others who have the same interests. You might have project reports, how-to guides, book reports, photographs or links to associated web pages.

Whatever you want to put in your web page, you will need three main items:

1 Storage space on the Internet to record the text and images that you want to share

2 Tools and facilities to help you assemble and arrange those components into the form of a web page

3 An Internet address that you can give to others so that they can view your web page

Your Internet Service Provider may make web space available as part of your Internet account, and provide the addressing needed. They would also provide or recommend suitable tools and techniques for building and publishing your web page. However, often the ISP facilities are limited to a predefined home page that may limit what you are able to achieve. Creating your web page at the ISP would also make it harder for you to switch suppliers, if your requirements were to change.

Fortunately, there are many other Internet services that will meet all of the requirements for building web pages. For some, it is their main business and they will require a monthly or annual fee, except perhaps for the initial trial period. Others, such as Yahoo may already be providing other services and will offer web page creation as an additional free feature.

Yahoo and GeoCities

The web building services offered by Yahoo are under the GeoCities label. You'll find a link at the Yahoo website, or you can go straight to the GeoCities website.

Featured Services
• Downloads
• Health
• Kids
• GeoCities
• Y! International

Don't forget

You use the same Yahoo ID to sign in to any of the Yahoo services, including web-mail, Flickr, Groups and Geocities.

1 Go to the website **geocities.yahoo.com**, and click the **Sign Up Now** button

2 All you need to access GeoCities is your Yahoo ID and password. Enter these and click **Sign In**

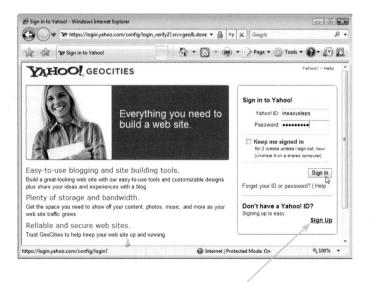

3 If you have not yet obtained your Yahoo ID, click **Sign Up** to enroll (see page 137)

Verify Registration

You are asked to complete a small survey, indicating the type of website you plan to build, and where you learned about the GeoCities free service.

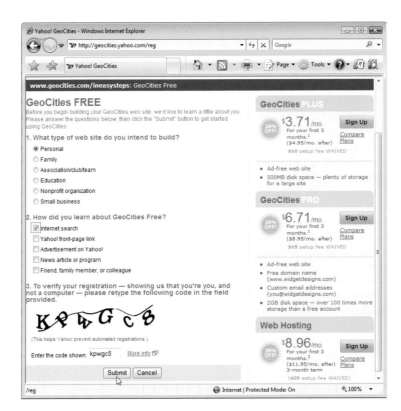

1 Click the buttons for your answers to the questions, type in the pictorial code, and click **Submit**

Your home page will be **www.geocities.com/your_id**, where **your_id** is your Yahoo ID (e.g. your_id@yahoo.com).

Create Website

1 Go to **geocities.yahoo.com/gcp** to display the GeoCities control panel. If you are not signed in to Yahoo, you'll be prompted to do this first

Hot tip

The GeoCities control panel is the center of operations, the console from which you carry out all the activities involved in creating and managing your website.

2 Click the **Create & Update** tab to get started

3 Scroll down to the **Basic Site Building Tools** section, with links to PageBuilder and PageWizards. We'll illustrate the process using PageWizards to create the pages and make any changes needed

Don't forget

More experienced users may prefer to use PageBuilder (see page 162). It is also possible to build web pages using tools on the computer, and then upload the files to the website server.

PageWizards

1 Click the **Yahoo PageWizards** link (see page 155) or go to **geocities.yahoo.com/v/w**

2 There are **About Me** pages in various styles, but scroll down to select **Personal Page** as your model

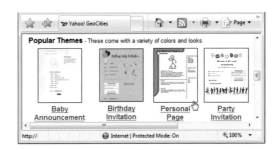

3 Click **Launch Yahoo PageWizards** and then click the **Begin** button

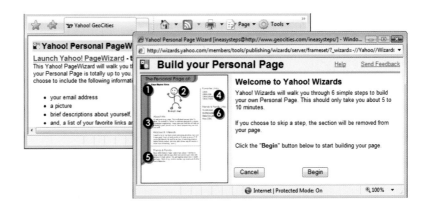

Build Your Page

Before you enter the contents for the web page, choose the color scheme you prefer, then click **Next**.

① Enter your name and your email address as you want them to appear on the website, then click **Next**

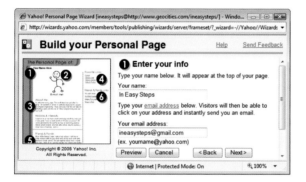

② Pick an image from your account, use the default image (or have no image, if desired), then click **Next**

Hot tip

There are six sections to be completed for the contents of the web page:

1 Enter your info
2 Pick your picture
3 Describe yourself
4 Enter your links
5 Describe family
6 Enter family links

Don't forget

Click Upload New Image to add a .gif file, or a .jpeg file (e.g. a digital photograph) to the list of images in your account, ready for you to select.

...cont'd

3 Type in brief descriptions about yourself and about
your hobbies and interests, then click **Next**

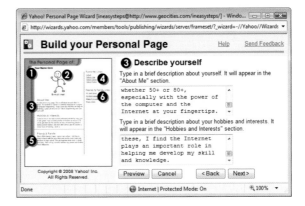

4 Provide a list of your favorite Internet links (names
and addresses) such as the examples, then click **Next**

5 Click **Next** and omit this section from the web page

6 The final section is for additional links. These can be used to extend the initial list, even if you didn't use the Family and Friends section. Click **Next**

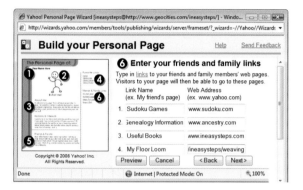

7 Type a name for your page. If it is the main page in your website it should be named **index**. Click **Next**

159

8 The **www.geocities.com/ineasysteps/index.html** web page is now complete. Click **Done** to terminate

View the Web Pages

Hot tip

It isn't necessary to type the file type .html. For the main page of your website, you can also leave off the page name.

Don't forget

To justify the free website facility, Yahoo has added what it believes to be relevant adverts. Click the tab to hide or reveal the ads, or upgrade to the chargeable service, to eliminate adverts.

Beware

The new page should have a home page link, and the home page should have a link to the new page, so you can navigate between them.

Since the PageWizards tool applies changes directly at the GeoCities server, you can view your new web page without having to transfer files or wait for updating.

1 Enter the address for the web page, in this case **www.geocities.com/ineasysteps** will suffice

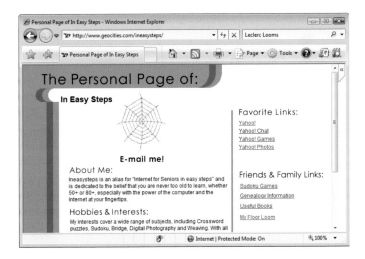

2 Create a second page for your website. In this case, we have created a web page called **weaving** which is at **www.geocities.com/ineasysteps/weaving**

Making Changes

You might decide to disguise your email address, e.g. replace **ineasysteps@yahoo.com** with **ineasysteps AT yahoo.com** (to thwart snooper programs searching websites for email IDs). You can make such changes using PageWizards.

1 Start the Yahoo PageWizards (see page 156) and select the appropriate type of template

2 Select **Edit existing page**, click the down arrow and select the page by name

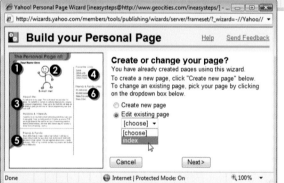

3 Step through the sections, making changes as needed and clicking **Next** until you reach the final stage and click **Done** to finish

Hot tip

There are programs designed to search websites for anything that looks like an email address, to add it to mailing lists used for unsolicited emails (spam). Making your email address less obvious can help protect you from this.

Your email address:
ineasysteps AT gmail.com
(ex. yourname@yahoo.com)

161

Don't forget

Clicking Next at the section where you name the page (see page 159) will cause your changes to be saved to the server. Type a new name to make a copy of the web page.

Using PageBuilder

Hot tip

PageBuilder gives you
more flexibility over
your web page layout
and content.

To make more comprehensive changes to your web page,
you should use the PageBuilder tool.

1 Click the **Yahoo PageBuilder** link (see page 155) or
go to **geocities.yahoo.com/v/pb.html**

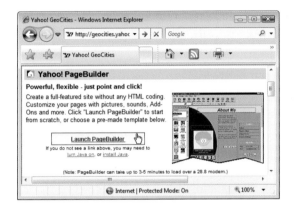

2 Click the **Launch
PageBuilder** button.
You may need to
disable the pop-up
blocker (see page 172) while
you edit your web pages

3 PageBuilder starts up, opening
a control window and then
the Java applet window itself

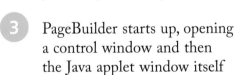

Don't forget

You must leave this
control window open
while you are using
the PageBuilder tool.

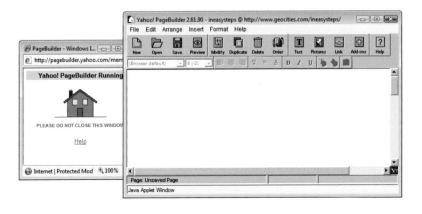

4 Press the **Open** button and select one of your web page files, in this case **home.html**, a copy of index.html

5 You are warned that your PageWizards file will be converted to the PageBuilder format. Click OK

6 The web page is opened ready for editing. You can for example delete a superfluous heading

7 Double-click a link to change the text displayed

8 Press the **Link** button to change the website address

9 Press the **Save** button, to complete the changes and then click OK to view the revised page

Beware

If you create a page in PageWizards, and then edit and save it in PageBuilder, you must no longer use PageWizards to edit that file.

Don't forget

There are many more changes you can make using PageBuilder. You can even enter html code, if you wish.

163

Blogs

People have always kept a daily journal. Samuel Pepys started his in 1659, and is famed for it to this day. Captain Cook kept a journal, as did many politicians. Even the fictional Adrian Mole kept a diary.

Today, everyone can do it, with the aid of the Internet and a web log, usually shortened to blog. This is a website where the entries are dated (and regularly updated) and displayed in reverse order, latest at the top. They have feedback systems, to allow readers to add their comments.

Style and taste in blogs vary enormously. To get a flavor of the range, view a variety of blogs.

1 Go to **blogsearch.google.com** and search on a topic

You will get a list of related blogs, if there are entire blogs dedicated to your topic, plus a selection of individual blog posts that are associated with your topic.

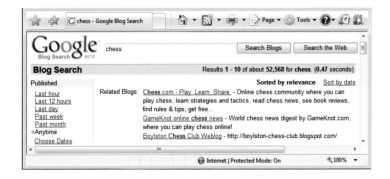

Create a Blog

If you'd like to try blogging, go to **www.blogger.com** and click the link **Create Your Blog Now**.

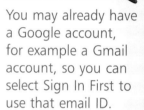

Hot tip

You may already have a Google account, for example a Gmail account, so you can select Sign In First to use that email ID.

1 Create a Google account, using an existing email ID

2 Specify your display name and click **Continue**. to sign up for Blogger using your Google account

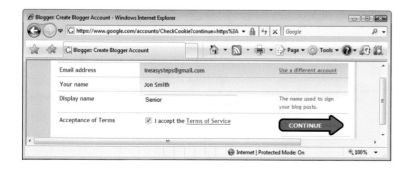

Post to Your Blog

The blog address is part of a web address for your blog, so it should be lower case letters, numbers and hyphens only. Check Availability tells you if the name is in use.

1 Name your blog and provide the blog address

2 Choose a template and click **Continue**

You can change or replace the template after your blog has been created.

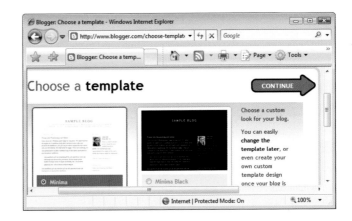

You provide the title and text for your post (blog entry) then click Publish Post to make it visible at the blog site.

3 Your blog will be created. Click **Start Posting**

RSS Web Feeds

Web feeds are summarizations of website changes, e.g. new headlines in CNN or new posts in blogs. There's a **Feeds** icon on the Internet Explorer toolbar. On some websites this is grayed (inactive). Hover over it and you are told **No feeds detected**. On other sites, the icon changes color and becomes active, and you can **View feeds**.

Hot tip

RSS stands for Really Simple Syndication, and is used to describe the technology used in creating feeds. Websites with feeds usually exhibit an RSS Feed icon.

1. At **www.cnn.com**, click the down arrow next to the Feeds icon, and you'll see two CNN feeds listed

2. Click an entry to view the feed at its website. Click **Subscribe to this feed** to get regular updates at your computer

3. Add this feed to your Feeds list in your Favorites Center

4. You have now successfully subscribed for updates of the chosen CNN feed

Hot tip

The Feeds feature is managed in the same way as your Favorites, so you can organize entries into subfolders, storing related feeds together under the same heading (see page 25).

View Feeds

1. To view your subscribed feeds, click **Favorites Center**, and then click the **Feeds** button

2. Select a feed from the list, to see the latest entries for that particular feed

3. Click the **Feeds** button as above, then click the arrow icon at the top right

4. Select individual feeds in turn from the list

12 Internet Security

You need to take care when you visit the Internet, since it has become a target. However, there are many ways in which you can protect yourself from risk.

Browser Security

Internet Explorer 7 in Windows Vista incorporates a series of enhancements to help protect your system from attackers. The features provided include:

● **Phishing Filter**
Analyses web page content and URL, and checks them against a list of questionable sites (see page 171)

● **PopBar Blocking**
By default, popup windows are blocked (see page 172)

● **Address Bar Protection**
Helps prevent malicious sites emulating trusted sites, by ensuring every window, pop-up or standard, shows an address bar and URL

● **Delete Browsing History**
Enables you to clear cached pages, passwords, form data, cookies and history, with a single click (see page 173)

● **URL Handling Security**
Redesigned URL parsing ensures consistent processing and minimizes possible exploits

● **Protected Mode**
This will run the IE process with very low rights, without express user interaction on your part

● **ActiveX Opt-In**
This reduces risk to your computer by turning off access to most ActiveX controls by default (see page 174)

● **Fix My Settings**
The Information Bar warns you when your current security settings put your system at risk, and offers to restore the settings to the default level (see page 176)

● **Windows Defender**
Constantly scans critical areas of the file system to ensure nothing compromises the system (see page 178)

Phishing Filter

The Phishing Filter is an opt-in feature, so is only activated on request. However, Microsoft makes sure that you are aware of it, the first time you visit a suspect website.

Hot tip

Even if you don't switch on automatic filtering initially, you can always click Check This Website to verify an individual location.

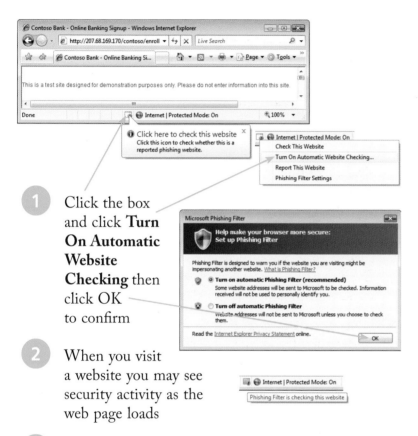

1. Click the box and click **Turn On Automatic Website Checking** then click OK to confirm

2. When you visit a website you may see security activity as the web page loads

3. You are advised of suspected or known phishing sites

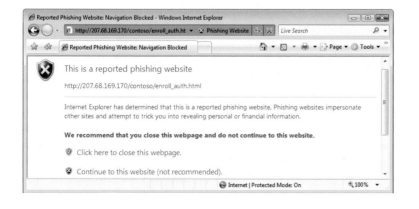

Beware

Be very sure of the website, before over-riding the advice from the Phishing filter, which is updated frequently to include new threats (and correct any errors).

Pop-up Blocking

The Pop-up Blocker is turned on in Internet Explorer by default and will block most pop-ups.

1 Visit the website **www.testpopup.com**, and select a pop-up style such as **Mouseover PopUp**

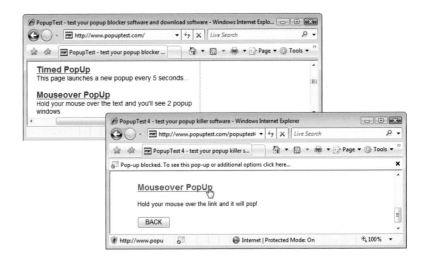

2 Move the mouse over the text as instructed and an Information bar message **Pop-up blocked** appears

3 Click the Information bar and choose to temporarily allow pop-ups at this site (for the current visit only)

4 Choose to always allow pop-ups from this site, to have them appear on future visits

5 If the Information Bar isn't displayed, click Tools, Pop-up Blocker to display the list of options

Delete Browsing History

As you browse the web, Internet Explorer stores details of the websites you visit and data that you type into web forms. The information Internet Explorer stores includes:

- Temporary Internet files
- Cookies
- History of your website visits
- Data entered into web forms
- Saved Passwords
- Temporary information

Storing this information is intended to improve your web browsing speed, but you may want to delete the recorded details if you're cleaning up your computer, or if you have been using a public computer.

To delete all of the browsing history:

1. Click Tools, and then click Delete Browsing History

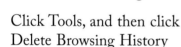

Hot tip

You can delete a specific category by clicking the associated individual Delete button.

173

2. Click **Delete all**, choose to delete files and settings for add-ons if desired, and then click **Yes**

Don't forget

Deleting all of the browsing history will not delete your list of favorites or your subscribed feeds.

3. Close Internet Explorer when the deletion has completed, to clear cookies that are still in memory

Add-ons

Internet Explorer asks permission before installing or running an add-on for the first time.

Hot tip

Add-ons are small applications that extend the browser (e.g. extra toolbars, animated mouse pointers, stock tickers). Often they come from websites you visit.

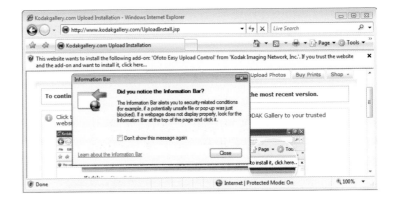

1 For example, the first time you **Upload Photos** to www.ofoto.com, (see page 126) the Information bar may tell you the website wants to install an add-on

2 If you trust the website, click **Close** then click the bar and select **Install ActiveX Control**

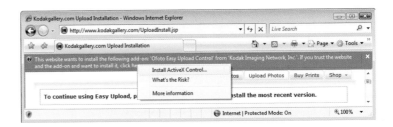

Hot tip

Internet Explorer has a list of pre-approved add-ons that have been checked and digitally signed. These are run without displaying the permissions dialog. They may come from Microsoft, your computer supplier or your ISP.

3 Click **Install** when the security warning appears, and the software will be added and enabled

If you believe that a new add-on is causing problems on your system, for example causing Internet Explorer to shut down unexpectedly, you can disable it.

1 Click **Tools, Manage Add-ons,** and then click **Enable or Disable Add-ons**

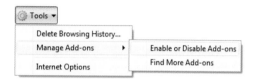

2 In the Show list, click the entry to show add-ons that have been used by Internet Explorer

3 Select the add-on you want to disable, and then click the **Disable** button. Click OK to finish

4 To reinstate a disabled add-on, select it as above, then click the **Enable** button, and then click OK

Fix My Settings

You can make changes to your Internet settings that result in your system becoming insecure. For example:

1 Click **Tools, Internet Options** and the Security tab, and click Custom Level. Select an option that is labeled as not secure

2 Click **OK** then **Yes** to change the setting

3 Internet Explorer now displays an Information bar warning and message as home page

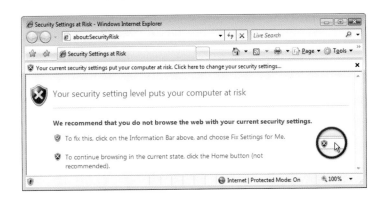

4 Click the Information Bar and select **Fix Settings for Me**

5 Click the **Fix Settings** button to confirm, and your settings will be restored to the defaults

Windows Update

1 Click Start, All Programs, Windows Update, or click Control Panel, Security, Windows Update

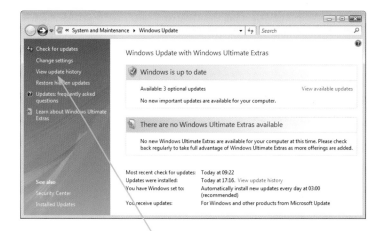

Hot tip

Windows Update provides you with online updates to keep your computer up-to-date with the latest security fixes.

2 Click the **View Update History** link to see a list of all the updates that have been applied to your system

Don't forget

Click Change Settings and choose Use Microsoft Update service, to receive updates for Office as well as for Windows.

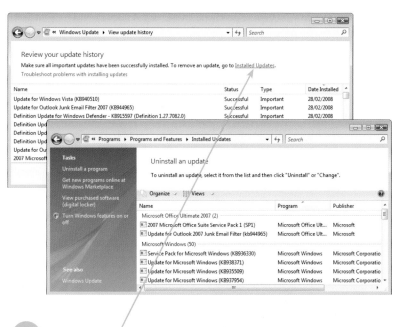

3 Click **Installed Updates** to view the important updates and, if necessary, uninstall selected updates

Firewall and Malware

1 Select Start, Control Panel, Security and then click Security Center

Security Center

2 Both Firewall and Malware protection should be On

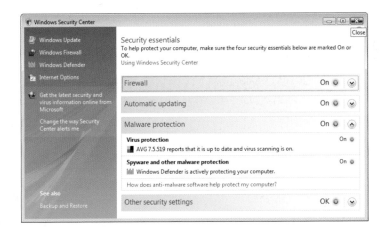

3 Automatic updating should also be On, if your system is connected via DSL or Cable

Windows Vista includes built-in Firewall software, along with Windows Defender to protect against spyware. There's no Antivirus software included in Windows. If no third-party product was supplied with your system, you can download the AVG Free Edition antivirus software from **www.grisoft.com** for personal use, or software from other suppliers including Symantec, Sophos and McAfee.

Website Directory

These are websites from across the world that are of particular interest to seniors, to help you continue your exploration of the Internet.

50 Plus Information

AARP
www.aarp.org

Originally the American Association of Retired Persons, AARP is a nonprofit, nonpartisan membership organization for people aged 50 and over, whether retired or not. U.S. citizenship is not required for membership.

CARP
www.carp.ca

This is the Canada's association for fifty-plus, and it aims to promote the rights and quality of life of mature Canadians.

Friendly4Seniors
www.friendly4seniors.com

An excellent resource, with over 2000 websites that are reviewed and approved as senior related prior to listing. You can search for sites by category, state or keywords.

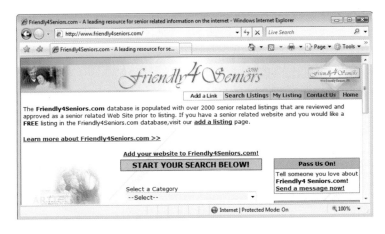

Silver Surfers
www.silversurfers.net

This was created for the UK, but does have an international flavor. It is an interface to some of the best websites for the over 50s, with links to over 10,000 – British and worldwide.

Don't forget

There's a website associated with CARP at www.50plus.com

Hot tip

The websites are mainly related US states and Canadian provinces, plus some international listings.

Communicating

Classmates Online   www.classmates.com

Classmates Online connects members throughout the US and Canada with friends and acquaintances from school, work and the military. Its Classmates International subsidiary operates in Sweden and in Germany.

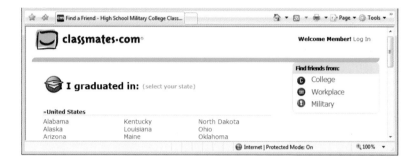

Hot tip

When you look back and realize how many people you have lost touch with over the years, perhaps you'll feel the urge to find out where they are now, and what has happened to them.

Friends Reunited   www.friendsreunited.com

If you went to school or college in the UK, the far East or Australasia, you may be able to locate some of your old classmates by registering at the Friends Reunited website for the appropriate country.

People Search   www.whowhere.com

If you want to track down an acquaintance, not necessarily an old school or army mate, this will help you find the latest phone number and address information, email addresses and contact data, or to find the name and address from the phone number.

Hot tip

The Lycos WhoWhere people search is just one of the many directory based websites that allow you to search for people (and businesses).

Digital Photography

Photographic Walks   www.all-free-photos.com

A collection of over 900 high resolution images of European walks and travels, panoramic views included, in galleries of castles and parks, towns and villages, landscapes etc.

Satellite Views   maps.google.com

At the Google Maps site, search for a location, for example the House of Commons in London, UK. Then click the Satellite button to view from above, zooming in to reveal as much detail as the available satellite photographs allow.

Tips   www.internetbrothers.com/phototips.htm

Visit the PhotoTips page at the Internet Brothers website for a selection of digital photography tips and tutorials. For example, there is a step-by-step guide on how to take a series of overlapping digital photos and turn them into a 360° panorama video.

Digital Photography
instant gratification

Learning

Elderhostel   www.elderhostel.org

Elderhostel is a not-for-profit educational travel organization providing short, on-campus courses for people 55 and over, with 8,000 offerings a year in more than 90 countries.

Hot tip

Elderhostel also funds the Elderhostel Institute Network (EIN), an association for Lifelong Learning Institutes (LLIs), which provide ongoing academic programs.

SeniorNet   www.seniornet.org

SeniorNet is aimed at computer-using adults, age 50 and older. It supports over 240 Learning Centers throughout the U.S. and in other countries, publishes newsletters and instructional materials, and supports online round table discussions at the website.

U3A   www.harrowu3a.co.uk/u3a_sites.html

U3A (University of the Third Age) is an international organization whose aims are the education and stimulation of retired members of the community. The Harrow U3A maintains a list by country of links to U3A and other institutes for learning in retirement.

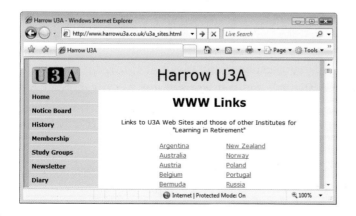

Don't forget

If you have skills and knowledge in any area, U3A gives you the opportunity to teach others and share your expertise.

Publishing on the Internet

Accessibility Initiative

www.w3.org/wai/references/quicktips/overview.php

Seniors know better than most, how web pages can become unreadable due to poor color, contrast, etc. This overview summarizes the key concepts of accessible web design (e.g. a site suitable for the visually impaired) as a set of quick tips.

Piers Anthony

www.hipiers.com/publishing.html

Piers Anthony (the writer of the Xanth fantasy series) and his blog-style survey of Internet publishers may be useful, when you finish that novel you've always meant to write.

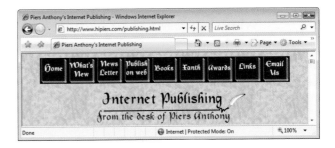

Weblog Awards

www.bloggies.com

This website tells you how to nominate weblogs for the various categories, gives details of the judging procedure and lists the finalists and the winning entry for each category.

Reference Material

GWR   www.guinnessworldrecords.com

Whenever you wonder what's the largest (or any other -est), you'll find the answer at the Guinness World Records site.

Merck Manual   www.merck.com/pubs

Merck makes available a series of online manuals, including the Merck Manual of Medical Information – Home Edition which translates complex medical information into plain language. There's also an online Merck Manual of Health & Aging

Maporama   www.maporama.com

Maporama is the most wide ranging mapping service, with maps for over 200 countries, and directions to and within over 60 countries including the United States, Canada, Europe, Asia and Australia. It generates routes with up to 3 stopovers, and you can specify road preferences

World Airport Codes   world-airport-codes.com

With almost 10,000 listed, this site provides airport codes, abbreviations, runway lengths, location maps and other information for almost every airport in the world.

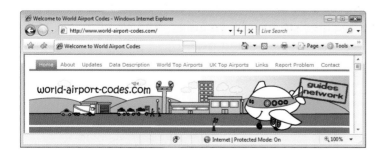

Hot tip

As this example shows, it isn't always necessary to enter the full website address. Here we omit www. but the browser still finds the website.

Travel

50plus Expeditions www.50plusexpeditions.com

Adventure trips designed and selected specifically for active travelers 50 and over who prefer smaller groups (16 or less).

French Waterways www.frenchwaterways.net

A different way to visit and explore France, and discover many of its hidden treasures. You will also experience gourmet cuisine, fine wine and unique sightseeing excursions to ancient villages, castles, cafes and markets.

OAG (official airline guide) www.oag.com

OAG is a global travel and transport information company which offers detailed airline, airport, country and city guides.

Saga Holidays www.saga.co.uk/travel

The Saga Group focuses exclusively on the provision of services for people 50 and over. These include holidays to worldwide destinations, from cruises to self-catering.

Hot tip

These are the holidays for those who enjoy the idea of activities such as wilderness trips, rafting on a jungle river or riding an elephant.

Don't forget

Saga also market insurance and finance products, there's a Saga Magazine and there are Saga radio stations.

Index

H

I

J

K